TO FIND THE WAY
OF LOVE

The Purpose Of Our Existence

To, Arthur and Barbara.
Old, old friends

Oliver E Dahan

Heroes for Young Readers and Heroes of History for Young Readers are based on the Christian Heroes: Then & Now and Heroes of History biographies by Janet & Geoff Benge. Don't miss out on these exciting, true adventures for ages 10 and up!

Christian Heroes: Then & Now
by Janet & Geoff Benge

Adoniram Judson: Bound for Burma
Amy Carmichael: Rescuer of Precious Gems
Betty Greene: Wings to Serve
Brother Andrew: God's Secret Agent
Cameron Townsend: Good News in Every Language
Charles Mulli: We Are Family
Clarence Jones: Mr. Radio
Corrie ten Boom: Keeper of the Angels' Den
Count Zinzendorf: Firstfruit
C. S. Lewis: Master Storyteller
C. T. Studd: No Retreat
David Bussau: Facing the World Head-on
David Livingstone: Africa's Trailblazer
Dietrich Bonhoeffer: In the Midst of Wickedness
D. L. Moody: Bringing Souls to Christ
Elisabeth Elliot: Joyful Surrender
Eric Liddell: Something Greater Than Gold
Florence Young: Mission Accomplished
Francis Asbury: Circuit Rider
George Müller: The Guardian of Bristol's Orphans
Gladys Aylward: The Adventure of a Lifetime
Helen Roseveare: Mama Luka
Hudson Taylor: Deep in the Heart of China
Ida Scudder: Healing Bodies, Touching Hearts
Isobel Kuhn: On the Roof of the World
Jacob DeShazer: Forgive Your Enemies
Jim Elliot: One Great Purpose
John Flynn: Into the Never Never
John Newton: Change of Heart
John Wesley: The World His Parish
John Williams: Messenger of Peace
Jonathan Goforth: An Open Door in China
Klaus-Dieter John: Hope in the Land of the Incas

Heroes of History

by Janet & Geoff Benge

TO FIND THE WAY OF LOVE

The Purpose Of Our Existence

Oliver E. Deehan

authorHOUSE®

AuthorHouse™
1663 Liberty Drive
Bloomington, IN 47403
www.authorhouse.com
Phone: 1-800-839-8640

First published by AuthorHouse 07/21/2011

ISBN: 978-1-4259-9851-6 (sc)
ISBN: 978-1-4634-4648-2 (ebk)

Library of Congress Control Number: 2011907591

Printed in the United States of America

For Barbara:

Always.

*The purpose of our existence
is to find the way of love.*

Contents

Prelude

In primeval times, our earliest ancestor looked at the night sky in wonder. Early civilizations used the stars in attempts to foretell the future. Then we developed telescopes, and our wonderment grew. We gradually learned we are part of a magnificent, radiant universe illuminated by trillions of stars clustered in billions of galaxies. We circle the center of our galaxy, the Milky Way, in an orbit that takes about 250 million years! And during the last century, we discovered the beginning of creation: "the Big Bang."

But we have questions beyond how the universe came to be and how it operates. We want to know how we relate to it. What influence does it have on our daily lives? Our home, in the solar system of a relatively minor star, is a small planet 4.5 billion years old. We are part of a glorious adventure—yet we have existed on Earth for only 200 thousand years. We alone among its creatures possess free will and a high level of consciousness.

As a consequence, and despite the insignificance of our position in the larger universe, we have produced some remarkable achievements. We have converted the Earth's physical resources into self-sustaining civilizations. We have advanced the health and longevity of our kind. We have invented language; created magnificent music, art, and architecture; developed mathematics and science to support astounding technologies. We have increased in number from a few thousand to more than 6.5 billion, and we have stimulated nature to produce enough food for those billions of people.

Yet, my observations of the world's societies are deeply disturbing. Despite all our achievements—despite the moral codes of great religions and the laws governing nations—cruelty, injustice, and every form of human misery have flourished for centuries. The average person has been continually and shamefully exploited, often in the name of religion, government, law, or "progress."

We allow millions of people to die of starvation every year and allow even more to live in poverty. We have not learned how to share with each other the abundance we have produced. And we have killed each other by the millions, not in popular uprisings, but at the direction of governments or religious institutions. Other creatures do not do this! We have not learned to live in peace. We allow politics and economics to trump our common humanity.

These problems, consequences of our successes, have existed throughout history and persist today, throughout the world and in most cultures. There seems to be a fundamental flaw in the way human society and its institutions are organized. There is a better way, the way of love. We need to find it for ourselves: we need to look again at the stars. For all our advances in civilization, it is disconcerting to realize that humans are the only species on Earth *not* evolving in harmony with the evolution of the universe.

Yes, we are on a glorious journey—all of us, together! There does not appear to be a specific destination. The purpose seems to be the journey itself. We need to better understand our place in the journey and how to make the most of the opportunities afforded us by the universe to create fulfilling relationships with our fellow travelers.

Oliver E. Deehan

San Miguel de Allende, Mexico

2008

Preface

The ideas for this book began to germinate about twenty years ago. They resulted from several life experiences, which together led to a reversal of one of my fundamental beliefs.

For the first thirty or so years of my life, I believed individualism was the most important element in living. Relationships were incidental. Personal values such as self-reliance, self-confidence, and individual effort were the values I wanted to live by.

My belief in the paramount value of individualism was supported and confirmed by current world events as well as my study of history. News stories almost always focused on an individual. Celebrities were always dealt with as individuals. Biographical details were not important in themselves—they mattered only insofar as they helped to define the celebrity's rise to fame. It was as though no one else was involved in the success of the individual.

History focuses on individuals whether they were monsters or miracle workers. And history tends to focus on physical force rather than the spiritual force of love. Genghis Khan, Dracula, and Adolph Hitler seem as important as Buddha, Christ, and Mohammed. A focus on individuals rather than relationships emphasizes self-interest over altruism, the sensual over the spiritual, and the differences that divide us. (Note the words *individual* and *divide* have the same origin.) A focus on relationships, however, modifies self-interest and restrains selfish behavior.

I first began to question my belief in individualism when I was in college. There, I began to develop an awareness of the common humanity of all people and the importance of relationships in and of themselves. Where before I had seen only two individuals, I now saw a third entity: the relationship between the individuals. Those personal values I had formerly focused on were no less important, but now I realized they are assets to be contributed to relationships. I also saw how personal values are shaped by relationships.

More questions about the primacy of individualism arose during my career as a hospital administrator and CEO. In that role, I had responsibility for results I could only achieve through relationships with physicians, nurses, technicians, and other healthcare professionals. I was none of these, and I learned that my greatest success came not through exercising authority, but through forming partnerships in which there was equality in the relationships.

Finally, after a divorce and ten years of active alcoholism, I joined the recovery program of Alcoholics Anonymous (AA). Through relationships with other recovering alcoholics, I was able to arrest my alcoholism. I experienced the power that groups and relationships have to restore individuals to physical and spiritual health. (In AA, the pronoun is *we*, not *I*.)

Most importantly, I came to believe in the spiritual

power pervading the universe. It is love, which is the manifestation of God's presence. Love impels, empowers, and sustains all relationships. It is available only to individuals and only to form relationships, which is why I *know* relationships are more important than individuals.

As my recovery progressed, I began to look for the reasons why relationships are so important. I have found some answers in recent knowledge developed about the creation of the universe, particularly in the work of Alan Guth, a physics professor at Massachusetts Institute of Technology (MIT). Guth and many other cosmologists contend the universe most likely appeared spontaneously out of nothing. He posited the significance of this theory for humanity: "I think it undermines the belief that we are here for any cosmic purpose. It does not mean our lives are meaningless. It means we must give meaning to our lives ourselves."[1] Guth also suggested that "rational thought, such as what cosmology brings to bear on the origin of the universe, could make the world a more peaceful place."[2]

For the merest fraction of a second after the Big Bang, quarks, leptons, and electrons floated independently in what Guth called "quark soup."[3] These fundamental particles make up all matter, from atoms to stars, planets, and our bodies. For the instant they floated in quark soup, there was chaos, as there were no relationships among the particles. But they were imbued with the attributes of freedom and equality. It is vital to understand that freedom and equality came into existence at the moment of creation, even before love. No particle was more important than any other, and none was controlled by another.

Then, science says, the four fundamental physical forces began to function—but it doesn't say why. Metaphysics says God infused the universe with the most powerful force, love, which was expressed as the four physical forces and which impelled the particles to form relationships, based on freedom and equality. That is the way of love. And thus, the evolution of the universe began.

Particles combined into atoms, atoms into molecules, molecules into compounds, and so on. The significance of this process is that the evolution of the universe consists of relationships continuously forming on the basis of freedom and equality. At any moment in its almost-14-billion-year existence, the universe could be defined in terms of the trillions upon trillions of relationships existing at that moment, then forming and reforming and producing entities of greater and greater complexity and diversity.

Among the qualities of being that we humans share, freedom and equality are the most important. They are deeper than instinct. They are qualities inherent in the fundamental particles that love impels to connect and to form relationships. They are of our essence, and they underlie our persistent struggle for freedom and equality throughout history. We are participants in a process that came into being at the moment of creation. It is empowered by love, which is the constant and universal presence of God.

In my readings and research, I have not found other authors who deal with this fundamental nature and importance of relationships, so I offer my ideas and discoveries in this book. It presents a universal and global perspective on the relationship between science and spirituality, which is love.

Chapter 1

Humanity's Inheritance

We are what we have been all along.

Humanity has been evolving for only 200 thousand years. (By comparison, the dinosaurs existed for 150 million years.) All that time, we have been following the wrong path. We exploited hierarchy and invented evil. Fortunately, this could not injure the universe. It can do just as well with us as without us, as it did for billions of years. But we have injured ourselves by believing in inequality.

This is shown by the imbalance of development in world cultures. Every day, increasing globalization in trade, communications, and travel reveals inequities around the globe. These inequities are expressed as limitations imposed on personal freedom and as inequality in personal relationships. They exist in government, politics, religion, business, economics, education, literacy, and health.

It is nearly impossible to find an area of human activity in which inequities do not exist. They are the consequence of corrupted self-interest. This book examines these inequities: how they came to be, what supports them, and how we, as individuals, can overcome them by focusing on our relationships in a new way.

The importance of relationships in human affairs cannot be overstated. There is implicit recognition of this importance in our role designations. When we say husband, wife, father, mother, daughter, son, brother, sister, aunt, uncle, cousin, niece, nephew, boss, employee, superior, subordinate, winner, loser, and so forth, a relationship is implied. Those words have no meaning outside of a relationship. This is true even with designations like prisoner and torturer, where there is inequality and one person controls the other. In all of these relationships, we, as individuals, must promote freedom and equality. That is the way of love.

To understand the way of love, we need to understand some important elements of our common humanity, starting with the fundamental and lasting ramifications of our common biological and physiological inheritance. As stated by John Brand,

> *Gray's Anatomy* applies to all of us. The sameness of our species transcends religious, political, ethnic, and all other surface differences. We all breathe the same air and die within minutes when deprived of oxygen. None of us can long exist without water. None escapes the reality of our biological common heritage. Just below the surface of our differences, we are all pretty much alike. All Indians and all Pakistanis, all members of Al

Quaeda and all CIA agents, all Republicans and all Communists, all people of all colors, religions, features, and languages will bleed when pricked and laugh when tickled, die when poisoned, and revenge when wronged.[1]

We are all governed (perhaps more than we'd like to admit) by the same five senses and the appetites they excite. These, combined with the power of speech, have been a major determining factor in the organization of civilization. Most importantly, evolution over millions of years has equipped us all with an amazing brain—a brain with three main formations that are interconnected but capable of acting independently.

The oldest formation, the basal ganglia (or reptilian brain), can be traced back about 240,000,000 years. The middle-aged one, the limbic system, seems to have first appeared during the Jurassic Age, about 180,000,000 years ago. The neocortex, the most recently developed part of the brain, is only about 3 to 5,000,000 years old.[2]

These three formations are referred to by neuroscientist Paul D. MacLean as "the triune brain."[3] It is important to distinguish the main differences between them because of their different influences on human behavior.

The functions of the reptilian brain are only concerned with survival of the self. The reptilian brain has been most effective in achieving that goal. While many species have been exterminated, neural reptilian circuitry has survived. Every aspect of the basal ganglia concentrates on the needs of individual survival. It has no concerns for other members of the same or any other species.[4]

According to MacLean, the reptilian basal ganglia even support cannibalism in premammalian life forms such as Komodo dragons and rainbow lizards.[5]

During the 60 million years following the development of the reptilian formation, the limbic system evolved. Science considers this brain formation to be the defining behavioral difference between reptiles and mammals. As astronomer Carl Sagan noted, "We share the limbic system with the other mammals but not, in its full elaboration, with the reptiles."[6]

With the development of the limbic system, early mammals were the first creatures to engage in parenting relationships, 55–65 million years ago. Parenting is a very important example of behavior that humans inherited from their earliest ancestors.

Clinical and experimental findings of the past forty years indicate that the limbic system derives information in terms of emotional feelings that guide behavior required for self-preservation and the preservation of the species.

There are reasons to think that the beginnings of altruistic behavior are in the limbic system. Indeed, with rare exceptions (chiefly the social insects), mammals and birds are the only organisms to devote substantial attention to the care of their young—an evolutionary development that, through the long period of plasticity which it permits, takes advantage of the large information-processing capability of the mammalian and primate brains. [Parental] love seems to be an invention of the mammals.[7]

Essential to parenting is an inherent prohibition against cannibalism as well as the ability to identify those to whom it applies.

> With the evolution of mammals there appears to have come into being the primal commandment: "Thou shalt not eat thy young or other flesh of thine own kind."[8]

Along with this instinctive commandment came the need to be able to identify "thine own kind." What developed was a process of fundamental importance to all mammals, but especially to humans. All mammals rely chiefly on vision to identify others as food, friend, or foe. So, one of my own kind is whomever I can visually identify as being like me.

To support this identification process, which I call "liking," our brain contains a special pathway between the vision center and limbic system, supporting our capacity for rapid recognition and reaction that is so important for survival. When the eyes see something emotionally charged such as a stranger, the information goes directly to the limbic system for evaluation (Is he like me or not like me?) and fast response (Do I kiss him or kill him or something in between?).

Like many mammals, humans also use their sense of hearing in identification. A similar pathway goes from the ears to the limbic system, enabling coordination of visual and aural information for emotional response.

This process of liking gives a new depth of meaning to the common phrase, "I like you," and it gives rise to the whole concept of liking the familiar and not liking the stranger. It supports positive relationships. Conversely, however, it can result in xenophobia, racism, bigotry, discrimination, and inequities of all kinds. Emotional responses of the limbic system can overwhelm logic, reason, or self-preservation, because the limbic system is older than these other areas of behavioral wiring.

After the development of the limbic system, the brain's evolution continued and produced the neocortex in another 175 million years. That was about 5 million years ago, when our earliest hominid ancestors made their first appearance in Africa. They were perhaps the first beneficiaries of this advanced brain capability. In contrast to other mammals,

> The neocortex enables our species to do a lot of stuff that other animals cannot do. It enables us to write poetry and to engage in ethnic cleansing. It enables us to discover the world of subatomic particles and to write viruses that can louse up the entire computer world. In our neocortex we make plans to build hospitals and find excuses to cheat on our income tax.
>
> Isn't our neocortex a grand thing? It provides the rationale to build and to destroy, to slaughter and to love. … Without conscious and intentional intervention, the neocortex can lead us down the road of doom. Yet willful management of our faculties gives us the chance to build a just society.[9]

Thus, each of us has a brain that will support our behavior—whether we judge it to be good or evil, because the brain itself does not recognize good or evil. Those are man's inventions. We make choices between them.

> The neocortex is oriented primarily to the external world and seems to serve as a kind of problem-solving and memorizing device to aid the two older formations of the brain in the struggle for survival. With its focus on material things, the neocortex develops somewhat like a coldly reasoning, heartless computer. It is the kind of computer that has the capacity to devise the most violent ways of destroying our own kind as well as other forms of life. *As though foreseeing that a terrible genie was in the making, nature enlarged that part of the neocortex, which for the first time in the world brings a sense of concern for the welfare of all living things. [italics added]* In the rapid progress from the Neanderthal to Cro-Magnon people, the human forehead develops from a low brow to a high brow. Significantly, the expanding prefrontal cortex underneath establishes connections with the third great subdivision of the limbic system— that concerned with parental care.[10]

This expansion of the neocortex does not mean humanitarian concerns will automatically triumph over the self-interest of the reptilian brain, but there is hope:

> In human beings, the neocortex represents about 85 percent of the brain, which is surely some indication of its importance compared to the brain stem, R-complex (i.e., reptilian brain), and limbic system. Neuroanatomy, political history, and introspection all offer evidence that human

beings are quite capable of resisting the urge to surrender to every impulse of the reptilian brain.

It is precisely our plasticity, our long childhood, that prevents a slavish adherence to genetically preprogrammed behavior in human beings more than in any other species.[11]

The brain came first and then came we. We are an effect, not a cause. Our brain is our most important inheritance from our earliest ancestors. For 240 million years, it has been developing capabilities such as artistic expression long in advance of the need or opportunity to use them—as if our brain has a brain, and has been searching for the perfect host.

We know evolution involves forces beyond our understanding, and here we are touching on the mystical and divine. We are evidently the brain's best host so far, but our self-destructive tendencies may limit our future value as a host. It behooves us to pay attention and try to understand what nature is telling us. Thankfully, there does seem to be a trend in the evolution of human societies to move away from selfishness and toward altruism. There is hope that we can create a civilization devoted to the common good of all people.[12]

The next thing we need to understand is how our relationships as living beings evolved, and how the freedom and equality governing relationships in the physical dimension are altered in the spiritual (living) dimension. Because of the food chain, in many relationships, freedom and equality do not exist.

Although we are part of the universe, we are not

essential to its functioning. Our 200-thousand-year presence on Earth is not a significant event in the larger history of the universe. All life, including our existence, is small and fragile. However, our direct physical connection with the creation of the universe is meaningful.

The Big Bang was a single event involving all of the matter and energy now existing. Since then, nothing has been added and nothing taken away. Matter and energy are constantly recycled. The cells of our bodies are formed uniquely for each new life, but as with all matter, those cells are composed of elementary particles that came into being at the moment of creation. We have new bodies on a very old chassis.

Our bodies also exist in both dimensions of the universe: the physical dimension of nonliving entities, and the spiritual dimension of all life. The first life forms, which appeared on Earth about 10 billion years after creation, were the first entities with the ability to reproduce. In addition, they had to eat in order to survive. The two basic forms of life—autotroph, meaning "self-feeder," and heterotroph, meaning "other feeder"—exist in a mutually beneficial relationship. Their survival is interdependent, and together, they make up the food chain.

Autotrophs feed on solar energy, carbon dioxide, minerals, and water. They produce oxygen and created the oxygen-rich atmosphere of the Earth, without which life as we know it would not exist. All green plants are autotrophs. Heterotrophs, however, feed on oxygen, water, and other organisms (including autotrophs). They produce the carbon dioxide that autotrophs need to live. All animals, including humans, are heterotrophs.

As far as we know, the appearance of life on the Earth was an utterly unique event. We are governed by the same imperative that has governed all life forms from that moment: namely, *life shall beget life*.* For higher life forms, this imperative has two aspects: self-interest and altruism—aspects often in conflict, forcing humans to make choices.

Self-interest involves behavior that enhances the individual's chances of surviving and reproducing without regard to the survival of another. To fulfill life's imperative, self-interest demands the individual eat and have sex. Relationships are only needed with others who are food sources or reproductive mates. Self-interest appears to have been the dominant motive in the behavior of living things from the evolution of the first animals through the reptilians.

For the progeny of those self-interested creatures, survival depended on an instinct for self-preservation. Cannibalism was common. Individuals of the same species did not help one another. Relationships were defined almost entirely by position in the food chain. Dominance, inequality, control, and self-interest were major factors in these relationships. Predation was essential for survival, and the predator had no interest in the freedom or equality of its prey. This self-interest, in combination with our senses and appetites, has exerted— and continues to exert—enormous influence on human behavior and civilization.

With the appearance of mammals, however, came the survival imperative's aspect of altruism. Altruism involves behavior that enhances another individual's chances of

---

* This imperative applies to each species as a whole, but not always to individual members. Particularly with humans, individual circumstances and lifestyle choices may preclude procreation.

survival and reproduction, even at the expense of the altruistic individual's own chances. Its expression always requires a relationship—and relationships exert a restraining influence on self-interest. But unlike self-interest, altruistic behavior asks nothing in return. It is the highest expression of a human being's unique capabilities.

The altruistic behavior hard-wired in the limbic system is amplified in the neocortex and prefrontal cortex. Psychiatrists Nancy K. Morrison and Sally K. Severino suggested this underlies our potential to "change ourselves to make our disposition of altruism more powerful than our dispositions of nepotism or egoism."[13]

The clearest expression of altruistic behavior in humans and their earlier ancestors is the care and feeding of children. On the savannahs of Africa, humans were more prey than predator. Having a child offered no advantage to the individual. In fact, raising children increased the chance of being prey. Children limited the mobility of nomadic bands. They required protection and a sharing of resources. Yet, despite the risks they faced, humans increased in number from a few thousand to more than 6.5 billion. This required a lot of childcare.

To understand relationships and the way of love, the final perspective we need is of the immense span of human history and its relevance to our lives today. Human history is measured in millions of years. It includes all of our inheritances, some back to creation (the impulse to form relationships), others to the beginning of life (the imperative to reproduce), and others to the appearance of mammals (extended parenting).

About 2.2 million years ago, the first true "man," *Homo*

habilis, appeared in Africa. He walked upright, made some tools, and then died out about 1.6 million years ago. But about 2 million years ago, *Homo erectus* appeared, also in Africa. He tamed fire and migrated to other continents, and his line extended to 400 thousand years ago, overlapping the appearance of the first known *Homo sapiens*—of whom he is most likely a direct ancestor. And after *Homo erectus*, the era of modern human history began.

As a product of that history, we need to know more about it and how it has influenced the relationships that define our lives. We attach great importance to our lives, and there is a temptation to believe we have escaped our origins—that we have invented the present. Most of us think of our personal histories in terms of two or three generations, back to grandparents or great-grandparents. In fact, our histories go back about 200 thousand years to the appearance of *Homo sapiens-sapiens*, the first true "humans."[14]

Each of us is linked to an unbroken chain of biological successes spanning about 12 thousand generations.[15] Think of it: You have a direct line of about 12 thousand female ancestors, and if any one of them had been missing, you would not be here. It took a vast number of couplings and an unimaginable number of people to produce you.

Our individual lives are an inheritance from all our ancestors. They gave us ways of meeting both our biological and our social needs. The biological needs and functions of our bodies and brains have changed very little over the thousands of years of human existence. However, our social needs, our behaviors and values, have evolved from the accumulation of layer upon layer of ancestral experiences. Each new layer was added to the previous ones, sometimes modifying the old but not replacing it. Changes in behaviors and values have always retained a link with the past.

It is very difficult to evolve by altering the deep fabric of life: any change there is likely to be lethal. But fundamental change can be accomplished by the addition of new systems on top of old ones.[16]

Thus, much of what we do today is in response to primitive biological impulses, modified by experience and intellectual development. For example, we still need to eat to survive, but over millennia we have changed our diets and improved our health and longevity. And nowadays, we eat for many reasons in addition to survival.

Also today, most of our relationships are contaminated by beliefs, established thousands of years ago, in the legitimacy of inequality and control. We inherited these beliefs, and they are so ingrained in our everyday lives that we accept these negative conditions without question, as the way things are meant to be.

Because we accept inequality and control, we support many institutions—especially governmental and religious systems—with a profound inherent flaw: they were organized as hierarchies after their foundation. This organization actually works against the achievement of their avowed purposes of promoting the common good, because hierarchy is one of the major functions of the reptilian brain, which is focused only on self-interest.*

---

* It is interesting that in the Book of Genesis, a snake, a reptile, led Adam and Eve into sin. "God created Adam and Eve in the beginning and he put them into the Garden of Eden. He created them in his image, perfect, without sin. The Lord then put the man and woman in charge of all things on the earth. The Creator gave Adam and Eve one rule. And the Lord God commanded the man, 'You are free to eat from any tree in the garden; but you must not eat from the tree of the knowledge of good and evil, for when you eat of it you will surely die.'"[17]

We have been struggling for thousands of years to overcome this flaw in the organization of human society without having specifically identified it. Now is the time to recognize that hierarchy is inherently flawed. Now is the time for us to work to establish new foundations for our institutions. The character of a civilization reflects the character of its people's personal relationships, not the other way around. This fact is unfortunately obscured by the influence that environment and existing conditions have had, and still have, on the individual.

Nevertheless, the organization of society is indeed an extension of the relationships between people. Where there is personal freedom, there will be political freedom. Where there is equality between individuals, society will treat individuals equally. So, where on Earth is there such a society of freedom and equality? It does not exist today, and it may never have existed.

Anthropologists have discovered evidence of a "relative" egalitarianism in our ancestors' hunter-gatherer bands and persisting in similar cultures today. The evidence shows that although equality was generalized for all members of the group, a hierarchical structure among males resulted from sexual competition, and equality did not exist in male-female relationships. For our future societies, the conditions of inequality, control, and hierarchy in both relationships and organizations must change. Fortunately, we have the power to make that change. It will require individual commitment and persistence.

We are really not far from the origins of those things that truly motivate us and govern our lives. We are just so influenced by our senses, achievements, self-interest, and where we perceive ourselves to be in the present that we ignore our cosmic connections—our relationship to the creation and operation of the universe. We need to focus on principles established at the moment of creation, which are valid and operating today.

Most of our beliefs and actions are based on ideas and behaviors inherited from the distant past. This book proposes some new ways of looking at our inheritance. They are ways that can support a more fruitful and fulfilling way of living than we have ever known. The goal is to support human activity on a foundation of freedom and equality. These attributes should be the first considerations in human relationships—instead of the unspoken belief in inequality and control underlying most human interactions today.

Each of us, alone, is free to define and adopt this way of living. No one can prevent it. It does not need gurus, priests, or leaders. No one need even know what we are doing, although others will respond in a positive way. It requires only individual courage and ingenuity.

At times people practice the way of love instinctively, even in extreme situations. One of the most powerful demonstrations is in the encounter of two strangers, Brian Nichols and Ashley Smith, reported in *TIME* by Andrew Sullivan as "When Grace Arrives Unannounced."[18] Under the direst of circumstances, Smith found the way of love:

> She went out for cigarettes. That's my favorite detail of the story told by Ashley Smith. It was not a noble calling; it wasn't even a noble errand. But the craving for nicotine at 2 o'clock in the morning apparently led Smith into the loaded gun of one

Brian Nichols, a man who was wanted for raping one woman and murdering another woman and three men. According to Smith, Nichols forced her into her apartment, tied her up, put her in the bathtub, and told her, "I'm not going to hurt you if you just do what I say."

What would you do under those circumstances? Scream? Panic? Beg? But at that point something else intervened. Smith actually communicated with her captor. She says she saw him not as a monster but as a human being. She talked with him. She told her story—how her husband had been stabbed in a dispute and had died in her arms; how she had then developed a drug habit, had been caught for speeding and drunken driving, had been arrested for assault (the charges were dropped), had ceded custody of her young daughter to her aunt. She showed him her wounds as a human being. And she saw in that man his own wounded soul.

It would be politically correct to describe that encounter as a spiritual one. But it seems to me it was more than that. It was, in the minds and souls of both human beings, an encounter with God. Smith's weapon, it appears, was a hugely popular book, *The Purpose Driven Life*, by Rick Warren. Smith says she read from chapter 33, which centers on the role of Christian service, on the idea that in every moment there is a chance to serve others.

Smith, blessed by what can only be called grace, saw that terrifying early morning in suburban Atlanta as one of those opportunities. Warren writes in that chapter, "Great opportunities to serve never last long. They pass quickly, sometimes never to return again. You may only get one chance to serve that person, so take advantage of that moment." Smith did. By her account, she talked to him, made breakfast, told him her story, listened. And as she revealed her openness to grace, so, apparently, did he.

He was an alleged rapist and murderer. She was tied up in a bathtub, clinging to the wreckage of a life that was barely afloat. One was a monster, the other a woman unable to care for her five-year-old, looking for cigarettes in the dark. And out of that came something, well, beautiful.

That was an exceptional moment of redemption. But every day we have smaller, calmer chances to turn another's life around, to serve, to listen. How often do we simply not see what is in front of us? How often do we believe that the world's evils—from terrorism to emotional cruelty—are beyond our capacity to change? Or, that there is no one in front of us whom we can serve? Smith and Nichols' story is a chastening reminder that we may be wrong. *[Reprinted with permission.]*

Smith tapped into a power available to every one of us. By her behavior, she promoted freedom and equality in a very bizarre relationship, and Nichols responded in kind. Their encounter demonstrated the enormous powers humans possess, and have used in the past, to adapt to and change their environments and life circumstances.

Each of us has that power. We call it love. It is the power of connection, of intimacy.

Everyone has an understanding of love—a personal, intuitive knowing. Love has no relationship to ego. Ego is a concept derived from our separateness, and it is a barrier to love. Ego supports reptilian self-interest. Love does not. Love supports relationship, as it focuses on the "other." It makes altruism possible. Many people equate sex with love, and sex can be an expression of love (or an act of control). But love is so much more. It is universal and always present. We can suppress it, ignore it, deny it, or distort it, but we cannot escape it. It is the cause of our being. It is God's greatest gift. *Love needs no laws: it is a law unto itself.*

Love is not only our nice feelings about other people. Romantic notions are only intimations of the vast power love truly is, for love is the continuing presence of God in the universe. The essence of love is connection. Love works in the spiritual dimension to impel relationships between living things, especially humans, in whom the physical impulse to relate is reinforced by free will.

Love is the "force" with which God infused the universe as part of the act of creation. It empowers and sustains all relationships in the universe, from those between elementary particles to those between people. Love will enable us to win the struggle to achieve greater freedom and equality in our relationships and realize our full potential as human beings. But to do this, we need to pay attention to some overlooked aspects of our history. We need to become conscious of our constant connection to our beginnings. We need to understand those elements of our inheritance that continue to influence our lives and behavior, especially self-interest, altruism, and our senses.

Chapter 2

The Development of Hierarchy

It all began with sex and continues to this day.

Human hierarchy is a concept founded on a belief in the legitimacy of inequality in human relationships. Hierarchy is expressed as an organization of activity in which individuals are assigned, and accept, positions of unequal power and status with limited freedom. It is a tiered, pyramid-like structure with power concentrated at the top. Power in this context is the ability of one person to control the behavior of another person.

Worldwide, hierarchies control institutions such as governments, religions, businesses, armed forces, and political organizations. Although hierarchies can be distinct from the organizations they control,* they are so pervasive throughout civilization that they structure

---

* For example, the U.S. House of Representatives is an organization of equals, but its members introduced hierarchies to govern it: namely, the House Rules and the rules of the political parties.

almost all human activity—and because of them, we have lost sight of our common humanity.

Within any hierarchy, occupants of the higher levels control the occupants of the lower levels, or possess more wealth, or control more resources. Among the many forms of hierarchy are:

- Autocracy—one individual holds complete, absolute power over others (also called despotism or dictatorship)
- Monarchy—a king or queen controls the distribution of power
- Oligarchy—power is vested in a few individuals who rule by hereditary right
- Theocracy—a dominant religion serves as the government
- Plutocracy—power is held by the rich
- Kleptocracy—rulers use political power to steal their country's resources
- Democracy—citizens govern by electing their government representatives
- Anarchy—a legal code is adopted by consensus, and no individual has power over another

Those forms have many variations. However, the essential characteristics of all hierarchies are the same: inequality between members and control of some members by others. Hierarchies also include patriarchies in families, especially as expressed in male-female relationships. In *Sex and Gender Hierarchies*, Barbara Diane Miller expressed these concerns:

We must not forget that human gender hierarchies are one of the most persistent, pervasive, and pernicious forms of inequality in the world. Gender is used as the basis for systems of discrimination, which can, even in the same household, provide that those designated "male" receive more food and live longer, while those designated "female" receive less food to the point that their survival is drastically impaired. Worldwide evidence shows that generally slaves, the poor, and females—not always exclusive categories—lead less comfortable and healthy lives than others.[1]

From the moment of creation, the process of forming relationships—that is, the evolution of the universe—was permeated by freedom and equality. But hierarchies are founded on inequality and control. At best they provide opportunities to collaborate productively. At worst they are directly or indirectly responsible for poverty, persecution, slavery, unjust imprisonment, genocide, terror, and despair. They kill millions. They limit freedom: freedom of speech, for example, is constantly under attack in hierarchies throughout today's world. Dominance destroys equality. Selfish satisfaction of individual wants destroys sharing relationships.

Finally, even nature's evolution is disrupted when human hierarchies assault the environment through deforestation, extraction and burning of fossil fuels, and water and air pollution. This assault will lead to the extinction of countless species, possibly including our own.

Why do we humans engage in and support these behaviors? Why do we utilize the divine gifts of freedom and equality to such a limited extent in building our relationships? Given that relationships are so important to the evolution of the universe and to our own survival, why do we diminish them in favor of the individual? Without male-female relationships, we would not exist: the relationship is more important than either the man or the woman. So how, then, did hierarchies become the dominant form of organization in human society?

Central to this book is the thesis that the creation of the universe was an act of God and that the evolution of the universe subsequently proceeded without divine control. From the moment of creation, the elementary particles had freedom and equality in forming relationships. Each was free to join with any other particle. Each had equal power and importance in the relationship they formed. It did not matter that they differed from each other. This evolution produced entities of increasing complexity and diversity. Atoms were made. The elements were created. Stars were formed, and stars collapsed. In the physical dimension of the universe, this process continues unchanged.

Where life exists, in the spiritual dimension, the evolutionary process is different. When life forms other than plants had to consume other life forms in order to survive, thus began the food chain, which introduced inequality and control into relationships. Self-interest became essential to survival. Not until the appearance of mammals and their brain's limbic formation did the capacity for altruism appear, first expressed as parental concern for offspring.[2] Before mammals, the closest thing to altruism was the production of progeny sufficiently precocious at birth to survive on their own.

The behaviors of the earliest humans, as for the animals preceding them, were largely governed by the self-centered drives for survival rooted in the brain's reptilian formation. These include aggression, territoriality, reproduction (sex), ritual, and establishment of social hierarchy. The human brain also had the limbic system's parental concerns, but during millions of years of evolution, the reptilian brain's tenacious self-interest established a primary influence over human behavior and introduced the fundamental flaw of inequality into the evolution of society.

This flaw first appeared millions of years ago when human bands lived out in the open on the vast African savannahs. Life was harsh. Humans were always in danger of being killed. In their constant search for food and their evasion of many terrifying predators, they faced daily challenges to eat and not be eaten. In "Nature's Prey," reporter Brian Deer noted, "It was not *aggression*, but *fear* which dominated our earliest lives."[3] In this environment, male dominance and patriarchy developed. We have inherited these patterns of behavior, and the impulses from our reptilian brain still exert a powerful influence in our lives.

Genetic evidence shows that all of our ancestors had their beginnings in Africa.[4] There they lived in small bands of five to eighty members. This lifestyle was essential for survival, as humans were prey and needed to live in groups to defend themselves. Fear was a strong motivation. Groups were also more efficient in finding food and caring for children.

The bands were nomadic hunter-gatherers. They had no spoken language until about 40–50 thousand years ago. They had no fixed settlements until 10–12 thousand years ago. Yet the behaviors of these bands have relevance for us today.

> Band organization is often described as "egalitarian": there is no formalized social stratification into upper and lower classes, no formalized or hereditary leadership, and no formalized monopolies of information and decision making. However, the term "egalitarian" should not be taken to mean that all band members are equal in prestige and contribute equally to decisions. Rather, the term merely means that any band "leadership" is informal and acquired through qualities such as personality, strength, intelligence, and fighting skills.
>
> The band is the political, economic, and social organization that we inherited from our millions of years of evolutionary history. Our developments beyond it all took place within the last few tens of thousands of years.[5]

As nomads, the bands did not produce any food surpluses. What food they found they ate. Their mobility necessitated minimizing any material possessions to be carried on their treks. As no individual could accumulate a surplus of resources, there were no significant material differences to support inequality. All band members, including children, fully shared their life experiences. They foraged together, hunted together, slept together. Their day-to-day survival depended on cooperation, not competition. The governing ethic was promotion of the common good. There was no slavery.

It is not surprising that male social dominance

developed during this period. The male's greater physical strength and endurance were valuable and necessary qualities for hunting game and effectively defending against predators. And within the bands, hierarchies arose among males. These were based on the dominance of males who were most successful in occasionally violent sexual competition for females.

From these hierarchies came the beginnings of patriarchy and male sexual domination of women. Anthropologist Barbara Smuts argued,

> Feminist analyses of patriarchy should be expanded to address the evolutionary basis of male motivation to control female sexuality. Evidence from other primates of male sexual coercion and female resistance to it indicates that the sexual conflicts of interest that underlie patriarchy predate the emergence of the human species. Humans, however, exhibit more extensive male dominance and male control of female sexuality than is shown by most other primates.[6]

Females resisted male domination, but as biological anthropologist Richard Wrangham and coauthor Dale Peterson described in *Demonic Males*,

> Ecological pressures kept females from forming effective alliances. With females unable to rely on each other, they became vulnerable to males interested in guarding them. Males seized the opening, collaborated with each other to possess and defend females, and started down the road to patriarchy.
>
> Males have evolved to possess strong appetites

for power because with extraordinary power males can achieve extraordinary reproduction.[7]

Our perceptions of life in the bands of *Homo erectus* and *Homo sapiens* are derived from anthropology, archeology, and observations of existing hunter-gatherer societies. We also learn from primates whose ancestors lived at the same time and place as our ancestors. Observing chimpanzees, our closest primate relative, is especially informative. Chimpanzees living today did not originate their patterns of behavior. These patterns evolved with their forebears and were inherited, and they reveal a great deal about our own evolution.

In the competition for power and status among males in the bands, males who achieved high status were rewarded with the only thing of value outside of food—sex. Higher-ranking males enjoyed more sex with more females. The emotional atmosphere surrounding sex was probably lust, not love; control, not collaboration. Pornography today probably depicts what the human sexual relationship was for millions of years. It was purely physical, mechanical, and aimed at male satisfaction. It was the reptilian brain at work.

Thus, sexual inequality between men and women became established in human society. Probably, at first, individual males sexually dominated females. Then males began to compete with each other for sex. A male hierarchy evolved based on sexual domination of females. This is not to say cooperation between men and women ended, which is obviously not the case. However, inequality between the sexes was—and is—a major inhibiting factor in the fulfillment of our potential as human beings. Patriarchy and hierarchy are products of this inequality.

The most important relationships in society are those between men and women, from which all others flow. It is tragic that the foundations of today's male-female relationships were laid very early in a chapter of human history based on male dominance. The pervasive inequality we inherited seems to have resulted from environmental happenstance—the practical values of male dominance combined with the sexual impulses of the reptilian brain. Inequality is not a natural human necessity. There are no biological or spiritual justifications for either male or female dominance. There are, however, both biological and spiritual justifications for equality (discussed later).

Two other factors in the primeval history of humanity that promoted the development and spread of hierarchy were common ancestry and migration. Because we are all descended from a small group of humans in Africa, the inequality between men and women established there became a common inheritance of all humans.

(Information in the following paragraphs is based on data from the National Geographic Society's Genographic Project.[8])

Along with inheriting the major behavioral characteristic of male dominance, *Homo sapiens* also emulated *Homo erectus'* migrations from Africa. *Homo erectus* is known to have traveled to Europe and Asia between 1.5 million and 600 thousand years ago, and then disappeared about 400 thousand years ago, just as *Homo sapiens* appeared in Africa. *Homo sapiens* migrated out of Africa for the first time about 200 thousand years ago and began peopling the world.

But the spread of *Homo sapiens* suffered a major setback

around 70–75 thousand years ago, in an environmental catastrophe of enormous magnitude. In Southeast Asia, at Sumatra's Lake Toba, a "mega-colossal" volcanic eruption occurred—the biggest of the last 2 million years. An incredible amount of ash was released in a huge plume, which traveled northwest and covered the area now India and Pakistan in a blanket up to 10 feet thick, with remains still identifiable today.

The ash in the atmosphere caused a six-year "winter." Global temperatures dropped as low as ⁻3°C and may have triggered a thousand-year ice age—the worst natural disaster humans ever experienced. Although the world population of the subspecies *Homo sapiens-sapiens* was reduced to 2–10 thousand survivors in Africa, they thrived, and genetic evidence suggests all humans alive today are descended from this small population.

In a second wave of migrations from Africa, humans colonized the landmasses of Eurasia and Oceana 40 thousand years ago, and the Americas 10 thousand years ago, replacing Neanderthal man and other inhabitants. Eventually, they spread all over the globe (except Antarctica). So today, despite many differences, everyone—French, Chinese, American—shares the heritage of our African origin experience.

Human migrations were astonishing accomplishments. Men, women, and children traveled hundreds or thousands of miles on foot into unknown territory. Few supplies could be carried, so food and water had to be found consistently along the way. It is hard to imagine what prompted such arduous journeys. Bands may have traveled great distances to find food or a more hospitable environment. Competition or violent encounters with other groups may have been a factor. Whatever their motives, human migrations carried inequality in relationships and interpersonal violence throughout the world. These were the roots of patriarchy and hierarchy.

About 40 thousand years ago, around the same time of their second migration from Africa, *Homo sapiens-sapiens* developed language. This was a huge leap in human evolution, and it may have been a major factor in the grouping of bands into tribes containing several hundred members. Language would have enabled bands to communicate ideas about cooperative effort. Then, as the formation of tribes produced the need for a more complex social organization than had existed in the bands, this would have accelerated the development of hierarchies.

Migration continued to have a major impact on the evolution of human society as, over thousands of years, the isolation of separate emigrant groups produced significant differences in culture, language, and appearance. The descendants of common ancestors in Africa became strangers to each other in far-off lands. No longer could the visual test of "like me" serve to establish kinship or friendship. And after hierarchies developed, these differences were exploited to support inequality and intergroup violence.

About 10 thousand years ago, agriculture was discovered. This and the emergence of language are perhaps the most significant milestones in the evolution of society. This was the beginning of civilization, and the beginning of the end for most nomadic cultures.

The daily, communal hunting and gathering of food gave way to organized farming by individuals and groups. Specialization and the division of labor developed. Relationships between individuals became more important and more complex than the previous relationships between individuals and the band. As cooperative activities were established, this led to the recognition of individual effort and the awareness of self-interest. Self-interest began to replace the bands' commitment to the common good.

Fixed settlements were created. Populations increased, as did the ownership and exchange of property. Men began to compete for material goods. Governments were formed. Male dominance over women was institutionalized. Slavery appeared.

Hierarchies flourished, and relationships within them became even more complex. Inequities in human relationships were legalized and became the governing ethos of human society. Hierarchies became entrenched as the dominant form of social organization throughout the world, and in them we lost sight of our common humanity.

Chapter 3

Hierarchies: Myths and Characteristics

Differences can exist between equals.
Hierarchies can exist only between unequals.

Men, not humankind, originated patriarchies and hierarchies. These are the structures that perpetuate the flaw in the organization of human society. Men built them on an ancient foundation of inequality in relationships. In these structures, the powers of ownership and control of people and resources are held by a single man or a governing elite, and women are largely excluded from governance activities. Patriarchies and hierarchies are created through threat or use of physical force.

As previously described, the impulse to create a hierarchy is rooted in the reptilian formation of the human brain, and primeval men acted on that impulse in their relationships with women and other men who acquiesced to the imbalance of power. This led to a fundamental error in the evolution of human society.

Patriarchy is worldwide and history-wide, and its origins are detectable in the social lives of chimpanzees. It serves the reproductive purposes of the men who maintain the system. Patriarchy comes from biology in the sense that it emerges from men's temperaments, out of their evolutionarily derived efforts to control women and at the same time have solidarity with fellow men in competition against outsiders. But evolutionary forces have surely shaped women too, in minds as in bodies, in ways that both defy and contribute to the patriarchal system.

Patriarchy has its ultimate origins in male violence, but it doesn't come from man alone, and it has its sources in the evolutionary interests of both sexes.[1]

The behavior patterns of patriarchy and violence, well established over the millions of years humans lived in bands, were spread throughout the world by the human migrations of 55–60 thousand years ago. And 8–10 thousand years ago, after the birth of agriculture, came warfare. Richard Wrangham and Dale Peterson cited evidence dating to 7000 BC in Jericho:

The stony remnants of that old city today tell us... Jericho was designed as a fortress: surrounded by one continuous wall more than three meters thick and four high, reinforced below by a broad moat cut down into the bedrock another three meters, supplemented above by a lookout tower rising an additional five meters. Written history starts a little later with scraps of pottery from modern-day

Iraq bearing witness to the Sumerian invention of writing around 3100 B.C. By then, the written record informs us, wars and the patriarchal systems fighting them were in full glory.

....But a sober waking reality suggests that if we start with ancestors like chimpanzees and end up with modern humans building walls and fighting platforms, the 5-million-year long trail to our modern selves was lined, along its full stretch, by a male aggression that structured our ancestors' social lives and technology and minds.[2]

Some say patriarchies and the hierarchies that followed them are what produced civilization and economic progress. This unwritten myth supports a widespread, powerful belief. True, our achievements as a species were produced under hierarchies. But there is no evidence that hierarchy itself was a causal factor in those achievements. Voluntary cooperation and creativity are more likely causes.

If hierarchy were causal to civilization and progress, the ideal society would have evolved long ago on a foundation of slavery, which was prominent in many ancient civilizations. The pyramids of Egypt and the Great Wall of China are examples of ancient works built by slaves. But society eventually turned away from slavery, not only because of its inhumanity but also because it proved to be uneconomical, as machines became more cost-effective for labor than humans.

Many other unwritten myths and beliefs support the concept of hierarchy. Educator Betty Reardon identified militarism and sexism as two such negative aspects of American society:

I believe that militarism is a value system which says that human beings basically need to be kept in order by force, and that some people have a natural right to use that force in order to do that. They're better equipped to decide what's best for the rest of us.[3]

This idea goes back to Plato. It asserts that humans are basically evil and that in order to have a just society, people must be made to act justly by the threat of force, or fear.

I think that militarism and sexism are in a way part of the same problem, and it goes back to the notion that human differences determine human worth, rather than having decided that the variety of human differences is just a rich kind of thing for us to exploit and enjoy. We've come to use human differences as a way of arranging people in a hierarchy of social and human value... And one of the other aspects is that human differences arranged hierarchically are so antithetical to what I feel is the natural way for humans to relate to each other that there has to be force to keep that hierarchical system in order.[4]

Ironically, the truth is that *hierarchies* must be *supported by* force or fear. Their production and distribution of benefits simply masks the nature of their underlying support. All hierarchies, in fact, create and rely on systems of rewards and punishments—the obvious carrot and the often hidden stick. Hierarchies could not exist without the stick, for two reasons.

First, our brains have no wired-in program telling

us how to relate to and behave in large groups.[5] Humans have to be "educated" to accept and support hierarchy as a means of filling the wiring void. Hierarchy provides us with rules of behavior. Do we cooperate or compete? The heads of the hierarchy will tell us. They emphasize the differences between people and use those differences to justify and sustain the inequalities hierarchies have created. Subordinate members are convinced it is in their own best interests to accept the system of rewards and punishments offered by the hierarchy. And this may well be true, when no alternatives are available.

Second, it is in the fundamental nature of humans to *want* to be free and equal in their relationships. Therefore, coercion is necessary to override this urge, which is even deeper than instinct. It is this urge that supports the struggle to be free and equal. We do not want to be controlled by others.

The statements above about militarism and sexism identify the myth that the people in the upper echelons of a hierarchy are superior humans simply because they occupy high positions, and are entitled to coerce or use physical force as they deem necessary to control inferior members of the hierarchy. They are also entitled to coerce or use force against other hierarchies. At best, this is competition—at worst, it is war.

Another myth used to support the legitimacy of inequality and control in relationships is accepted by billions of people around the world. It is depicted as a "divine pyramid," with God at the top and descending levels below: man, woman, child, animal, and all others. Power is distributed from the top downward in diminishing amounts. Occupants of each level have the power to control only those in the levels below them and are controlled by those in the levels above.

Obviously, men devised the pyramid. It is based on the theories of Saint Augustine, which attempted to legitimize medieval monarchies and were further amplified by Jacques-Benigne Bossuet's seventeenth-century doctrine of the Divine Right of Kings.

Although history and common sense today attest to the pyramid's falsity, many people still position themselves in society accordingly—lower, middle, or upper class, for example—and adopt its implicit inequalities in many of their relationships—thinking, for example, "My boss is better than me." This is an illustration of how people tacitly accept and legitimize hierarchies. Because hierarchies control the livelihoods of vast numbers of people, those people have a vested interest in their hierarchy's survival, even if they disagree with its goals or behavior.

The most important governing principle in a hierarchy's operation is *the hierarchy must survive*. In actuality, this means, "The top echelon must survive," because that echelon's members identify their interests as being above those of the organization they control. They are often willing to subvert or even sell the organization if it serves the interests of the hierarchy. Pursuit of the organization's original purpose becomes incidental, except as it may be essential in generating the financial and other resources needed for the hierarchy to survive.

This is the personalization of power, when top individuals in the hierarchy take the powers of the organization unto themselves. We witnessed a frightening example in the administration of President George W. Bush. He placed himself above the law with respect to civil liberties and torture; he defied the will of the

American people in pursuing the war in Iraq; and he repeatedly placed himself above Congress with his "signing statements," identifying legislation he disagreed with and proposed to ignore.

Personalization of power is a particular problem in the hierarchies of business corporations. In 1932, Adolph Berle and Gardiner Means identified and cautioned against it in *The Modern Corporation and Private Property*.[6] They documented that as corporate ownership becomes more diffuse through stock ownership, corporate management becomes more powerful and takes over many of the traditional functions of ownership. This is to the detriment of corporate and shareholder interests. Corporate wealth is diverted to private pockets. Corporate boards and CEOs become self-serving, as demonstrated by the many recent financial and corporate scandals in the United States.

While these men may applaud their own efforts, it may be ego-deflating to realize their behaviors are simply modern expressions of the primeval impulses of the reptilian brain. In the words of John Brand, "When controlling alphas decide that the fiscal bottom line is the be-all and end-all of corporate responsibility, when politicians decide that in the name of capitalism even inhumane decisions are acceptable, then reason and logic cannot prevail. Money and power are simply modern adaptations of the territorial imprint in the R-complex."[7]

Many corporate CEOs put personal compensation ahead of the bottom line, even when the corporation is failing. "No self-correcting mechanisms exist among the divisions of the triune brain. Self-limiting neural ganglia do not exist to put a stop to self-centered drives."[8] That power exists in relationships, which impose checks and balances.

The next most important governing principle is *the organization that is controlled by a hierarchy must grow.* It is in the nature of hierarchy to centralize power, wealth, and control. Historically, governments achieved these goals through brutal conquest, exploration, and colonization. Religions expanded by supporting governments and following in the wake of their brutal escapades. Businesses also supported and followed governments. In addition, businesses grew through mergers and acquisitions.

Too often, the threat or actual use of force has been employed in the growth of a hierarchical organization. Colonization is a prime example of this principle in action. The ultimate expression of the inequality of hierarchy is a society based on slavery, of which there have been many in human history. As anthropologist Jared Diamond noted,

> In ancient civilizations, many, perhaps most, early states adopted slavery on a much larger scale than did chiefdoms. That was not because chiefdoms were more kindly disposed toward defeated enemies but because the greater economic specialization of states, with more mass production and more public works, provided more uses for slave labor. In addition, the larger scale of state warfare made more captives available.[9]

More modern times have seen the American experience with slavery as well as the British, French, Portuguese, Dutch, and Spanish colonial societies, among others. States monopolize the use of force and back the interests of their friendly allies. Hierarchy has always been associated with violence: they are companions in the reptilian part of our brain.

As hierarchies grow, they begin to exhibit additional negative characteristics inherent in any organization founded on inequalities in relationships. The top echelon becomes isolated from the rest of the organization. This is due in part to decisions made by that group. It regards itself as an elite class with an exclusive membership. Its members exempt themselves from most rules governing the rest of the organization. They become secretive about their activities.

Furthermore, hierarchies tend to foster selfishness in individual relationships. Hierarchical relationships may be between two people or between groups, organizations, or countries. In every case, selfishness is a corruption of one side's legitimate self-interest. It goes beyond satisfying one's needs to satisfying one's wants by diminishing the freedom and equality of the other in the relationship. It does not have to be this way.

Alternatives to hierarchical relationships are described later. For now, I will examine hierarchies as they exist today. First, in defining the concept of freedom and equality in a relationship of two parties, these are measured by the degree to which each party has power *in the given relationship*. In a free and equal relationship, there is an equal balance of power. Each party has the power to decide if the relationship will exist or not. Both have equal power in decisions affecting their individual and mutual interests. There is no coercion. Punishment is unacceptable in resolving conflicts. Perhaps this describes an ideal, but it is achievable if each party sees the other as free and equal. Equality of circumstance may be impossible, but in a relationship of freedom and equality, either party's power outside the relationship is irrelevant.*

In the world today, each of us belongs to several hierarchies. We are citizens of a country. We are members of a church. We work for a corporation. We are in a labor or professional union. We meet with a social club. We are on an athletic team. We are part of a family…and the list goes on. Our relationships within each hierarchy are

---

* An anecdote may help to illustrate. I was serving as an officer aboard the USS Coral Sea when it arrived at Istanbul, Turkey, in 1951. The ship was at anchor in Istanbul's harbor and had two gangways over the starboard side for personnel to board. Standing watch on the enlisted men's gangway toward the stern, I witnessed the following event at the forward gangway, which was for officers and VIPs. A self-propelled scow loaded with fresh produce set out from shore, obviously bringing supplies, which we normally took aboard on the port side, opposite the gangways. But the scow was moving toward the forward gangway. A man, a Turk, stood in the bow, directing the scow's movement. As it approached the gangway, the ship's officer of the deck called through his bullhorn, "No, no. Go to the port side." The Turk did not respond, and the scow approached closer. The officer repeated his instruction. By now, the Turk was close enough to be heard without a bullhorn. He called to the officer, in perfect English, "I want to speak to your captain." The officer replied, "No, take your boat to the port side." A dialogue followed. Turk: "Are you the captain of that ship?" Officer: "No." Turk: "Well, I'm the captain of this one, and I want to speak to your captain." At this point, in keeping with longstanding seagoing tradition, the officer called for the ship's captain, who appeared and greeted his fellow captain. There could not have been a greater difference in their circumstance—one commanding a powerful warship, the other master of a boat that would not survive the open sea. But for the moment, they shared a free and equal relationship. Differences can exist between equals. Hierarchies can exist only between unequals.

different. But our position in each hierarchy determines the amount of freedom and equality we may enjoy.

Human civilization has been a work in progress for only 10 thousand years. As seems true for the universe as a whole, there is no defined end point toward which civilization on Earth is evolving. But assuming that a primary intention of civilization is to enhance the lives of all people, it is fair to examine the impacts hierarchies have had on the achievement of this intention, as well as the nature of these impacts. Hierarchies have been so dominant in human affairs throughout history, they can be judged as fully accountable for the world's evils.

My examination here focuses on several major elements of civilization: population growth, wealth production and distribution, governments and law (including the armed forces), religion and moral codes, literacy and education, the position of women in hierarchies, and hierarchies' impacts on their members (especially women) of both high and low estate.

Population growth. Perhaps our greatest achievement as a species is our growth in number. From several thousand couples in Africa 60 or 70 thousand years ago, we have increased to 6.6 billion people. Despite droughts, famines, plagues, ice ages, and wars, we have overwhelmingly fulfilled the imperative that life shall beget life.

Hierarchy deserves no credit for this. Credit belongs to humans for successfully mating and parenting. In this achievement, men and women are equal partners, even when there was inequality in sexual relationships and male dominance led to coercive actions ranging from "gentle" persuasion to the horrors of rape. Hopefully, in a society free of hierarchy, men and women will regard procreation and parenting with awe for the miracles they really are.

Our growth in number demonstrates the greater power of altruism over selfishness. It may also be one of the greatest problems facing us in the near future.

Wealth production and distribution. The wealth of nations rests on a reliable food supply. Thus, agriculture is the foundation of civilization. The development of agriculture has been a momentous achievement. How else would we feed the billions of people on Earth? Of course, the problem is, we don't. We allow more than 9 million people, including 5 million children, to die of starvation every year; 50 percent of the world population is malnourished; 1.2 billion have hunger; 2–3.5 billion have vitamin and mineral deficiencies.

Hierarchies are to blame. World governments could solve the hunger problem by taking a cooperative approach, but they don't. They even allow surplus food to be thrown away instead of finding ways to distribute it to those in need. Because they are focused on the selfish interests of their governing elites, world governments are not paying enough attention to worldwide environmental degradation and especially the deterioration of agricultural assets, which will seriously threaten future food production.

Our civilization has produced vast wealth by exploiting the development of astounding technologies, from the wheel to the computer, but it has also produced extreme maldistribution. Hierarchies promote the inequitable distribution of wealth, leading to the increasing concentration of wealth and power in the hands of fewer people. This began between 3.5 and 10 thousand years ago with government control of the production and distribution of food, as illustrated in the history of Sumer, the world's first recorded civilization.

Even the earliest Mesopotamian states exercised centralized control of their economies. Their food was produced by four specialist groups (cereal farmers, herders, fishermen, and orchard and garden growers), from each of which the state took the produce and to each of which it gave out the necessary supplies, tools, and foods other than the type of food that this group produced.[10]

Hierarchies divide humanity into haves and have-nots, and the gap is widening. Three billion people, nearly half of the world's population, live on less than $2 a day, with 80 percent in substandard housing. A billion children live in poverty, which kills 6 million of them every year. In the United States in 1995, the wealth of the top 1 percent was greater than the total wealth of the bottom 95 percent. The income disparity between the world's richest 20 percent and poorest 20 percent went from 30:1 in 1960 to a whopping 74:1 in 1997. And today, 6 percent of the world's population possesses 59 percent of the world's wealth.[11]

When government hierarchies allow these conditions to exist, they are not always acting alone. Most often, the wealthy and powerful act as their senior partners. Governments engage in massive transfers of wealth from commoners to the very wealthy. Commentator Bill Moyers spoke of this process in the United States, perhaps the world's wealthiest nation:

For years now a small fraction of American households have been garnering an extreme concentration of wealth and income while large corporations and financial institutions have obtained unprecedented levels of economic and political power over daily life. In 1960, the gap in terms of wealth between the top 20% and the bottom 20% was 30-fold. Four decades later it is more than 75-fold.

…The middle class and working poor are told that what's happening to them is the consequence of Adam Smith's "Invisible Hand." This is a lie. What's happening to them is the direct consequence of corporate activism, intellectual propaganda, the rise of a religious orthodoxy that in its hunger for government subsidies has made an idol of power, and a string of political decisions favoring the powerful and privileged who bought the political system right out from under us.[12]

Karl Marx correctly perceived the inequality of the prevailing economic system, but he failed to see the root of the problem was the organization of society by hierarchies. His proposed solution simply substituted one hierarchy for another. It does not matter what form of hierarchy prevails in a society: theocracy, monarchy, dictatorship, democracy—inequality is inherent in them all.

Democracy does happen to be the form of social organization with the greatest potential to evolve into a new form of society not founded on inequality. I call it simply "the new society" (described in chapter eight). But it must be a true democracy, not simply a government with free elections. There must be a body of law that recognizes and protects *all* citizens and their property equally.

Literacy and education. We invented languages and developed education systems, which are essential to human progress—yet, 70 percent of the people in the world cannot read or write. Only 1 percent have a college education. Public education systems are the responsibility of governments, but the education of students seems to get lost in the mazes of the bureaucratic (hierarchical) superstructures. Pressures for conformity increase and schools become regressive instead of creative.

Religions and moral codes. Great religions have been established and moral codes proffered to guide us in our relationships with each other, but they seem more to divide than unite us, and to consist more of prohibitions than positive propositions (these are left to poets and philosophers). Prohibitions do not work well. Doctrines become dogma, and the pressure for conformity escalates—witness the present rigidity of fundamentalists in the United States and the Islamic extremism in the Middle East. The existence of hierarchy in religions is antithetical to their avowed purposes of freedom and equality under God. As described by journalist Laurie Goodstein,

> This is a rare moment in history, like a planetary alignment: three world religions are simultaneously wracked by crisis. Roman Catholics learned that some of the princes of their church protected priests that sexually abused children. Muslims have seen their scholars condemned and their scriptures deconstructed for signs that Islam encourages terrorism. Jews in Europe have suffered a wave of anti-Semitic attacks as world opinion has hardened toward Israel.
>
> The nature of the trouble for each is different, but adherents of all three feel suddenly embattled and isolated. Atheists say, "I told you so," and even

> some people of faith are asking whether there isn't
> something in the nature of religion itself that ends
> in corruption.[13]

That "something" is hierarchy. Hierarchies create and support dogma, which only the governing elite has the power to change.

Governments, laws, and the military. Governments have been established covering everyone in the world. In them is represented the most advanced development of the concept of hierarchy. The freedom and equality of their citizens is always limited. In extreme cases, citizens are subject to torture, murder, slavery, arbitrary imprisonment, and execution. This is true more in dictatorships than democracies, but democracies are not innocent of these abuses.

During the millions of years our forebears lived in bands, survival and progress depended on the behavior of all band members in promoting the common good. It was the governing ethic of primitive society. Admittedly, during that period of human history, "the greatest possible good for the greatest possible number of individuals" was simple: it meant mutual protection and the sharing of food.

Only after the discovery of agriculture and the production of food surpluses, which supported the creation and proliferation of hierarchies, was the concept of the common good subordinated to the self-interests of powerful individuals. These individuals were able to create and maintain hierarchies through the use of physical force and the creation of laws to support the inequities that developed in agrarian societies. These were the leaders of chiefdoms.

In his brilliant work, *Guns, Germs, and Steel*, Diamond characterized the general actions of government hierarchies:

> Chiefdoms arose around 5500 B.C. in the Fertile Crescent...and chiefdoms introduced the dilemma fundamental to all centrally governed, non-egalitarian societies. At best, they do good by providing expensive services impossible to contract for on an individual basis. At worst, they function unabashedly as kleptocracies, transferring net wealth from commoners to upper classes. These noble and selfish functions are inextricably linked.
>
> What should an elite do to gain popular support while still maintaining a more comfortable lifestyle than commoners? Kleptocrats throughout the ages have resorted to a mixture of four solutions:
>
> 1. Disarm the populace and arm the elite. That's much easier in these days of high-tech weaponry produced only in industrial plants and easily monopolized by an elite [e.g., the military-industrial complex].
> 2. Make the masses happy by redistributing much of the tribute received [i.e., taxes], in popular ways. This principle was as valid for Hawaiian chiefs as it is for American politicians today.
> 3. Use the monopoly of force to promote happiness, by maintaining public order and curbing violence.
> 4. The remaining way for kleptocrats to gain

public support is to construct an ideology or religion justifying kleptocracy. Besides justifying the transfer of wealth to kleptocrats, institutionalized religion brings two other important benefits to centralized societies. First, shared ideology or religion helps solve the problem of how unrelated individuals are to live together without killing each other—by providing them a bond not based on kinship. Second, it gives people a motive, other than genetic self-interest, for scarifying their lives on behalf of others. At the cost of a few society members who die in battle as soldiers, the whole society becomes much more effective at conquering other societies or resisting attacks... The official religions and patriotic fervor of many states make their troops willing to fight suicidally.[14]

Government leaders and leaders of religious hierarchies, such as Christian and Islamist fundamentalists, often exploit fear and anger (e.g., the United States after 9/11, and Islamists after the invasion of Iraq). They use these primal responses to life events to shift our attention away from their actions that undermine the common good and to mask the advance of their own goals of personal aggrandizement and wealth transfer to the wealthy.

The government's monopoly on the use of force confers on them the responsibility for national defense. This supports the organization of the armed forces, which may dominate a government or be used by a government to wage war against other hierarchies. Today, homicide (through war and assassinations) and genocide are major factors in the competitions between governmental hierarchies. For these, commoners pay in blood and money—but not necessarily the elite, many of whom may instead profit from war. And these evils of killing are uniquely human. Other species do not massacre their own or other species.

Hierarchies often compete for control of more people and wealth. These competitions can be peaceful, as with most trade negotiations, but too often they involve violence, as with the Arab/Israeli conflicts. When one hierarchy challenges another, the outcome is either another hierarchy or an accommodation between the two.

An example of accommodation is the competition during the Middle Ages between the Roman Catholic Church and the rising nation-states of Europe. They agreed to share jurisdiction over the populace, especially in matters of taxation and tithing. They also cooperated in the Inquisition, one of history's most evil partnerships. Revolutions, on the other hand, often entail the replacement of one hierarchy with another. In France, the monarchy was replaced by a republic, then another, and another. Russia's czarist regime was replaced first by a democracy, in turn overthrown by a Communist dictatorship.

Hierarchies tend to be exclusive, shutting people out, labeling, stereotyping, scapegoating, to justify social inequality. They encourage secrecy in relationships and the withholding of information. Few stand out as champions of freedom and equality in either political or personal relationships.

The holders of power do not want to share it. They want to increase it. They can and will use all manner of means—intimidation, economic blackmail (job loss), dishonesty, and governmental manipulation—to maintain and aggrandize their superior positions and wealth. They identify more and more with each other. A sense of entitlement develops, along with communication gaps between those in power and the rest of the organization. Members of the top echelon hide behind the anonymity of the organization. They hold authority but resist and evade accountability. They become alienated from their subordinates.

Hierarchies often exercise strict control over the actions and movements of their members. Rulers such as Robert Mugabe of Zimbabwe and the military junta in Myanmar can prevent the outside world from intruding and prevent their citizens from exiting the country or communicating with the outside world.

Hierarchies produce laws and codes setting forth rules on how to behave in society. However, leaders often exempt themselves from these rules. They use the impersonal nature of their organizations to shield themselves from public responsibility and accountability for their actions. They develop systems of rewards and punishments—the heart and soul of the authoritarian organization—to sustain inequality and control. These are backed up by the legal system and perpetuate inequality in relationships.

The systems of law instituted in hierarchies are basically adversarial. Laws passed are under constant challenge from those who want to expand governmental control over people and property as well as those who want to reduce it. Laws become the raw material used by lawyers to produce evasions and exceptions for members of hierarchies' upper echelons. Governments accede to pressures to benefit the elite members of their constituencies. The actions of hierarchies bring into being laws to support their existence and other laws to curb their excesses.

The United States is a leading world democracy, perhaps the best. Yet, as pointed out by journalists Donald L. Bartlett and James B. Steele, even the best of governments is susceptible to contamination from the underpinnings of inequality and control inherent in all hierarchies.

> When powerful interests shower Washington with millions in campaign contributions, they often get what they want. But it's ordinary citizens and firms that pay the price—and most of them never see it coming
>
> …This is what happens [if you don't contribute to their campaigns or spend generously on lobbying]:
> - You pick up a disproportionate share of America's tax bill.
> - You pay higher prices for a broad range of products, from peanuts to prescription drugs.
> - You pay taxes that others in a similar situation have been excused from paying.
> - You are compelled to abide by laws while others are granted immunity from them.
> - You must pay debts that you incur while others do not.
> - You are barred from writing off on your tax returns some of the money spent on necessities while others deduct the cost of their entertainment.
> - You must run your business by one set of rules

while the government creates another set for your competitors.

...The fortunate few who contribute to the right politicians and hire the right lobbyists enjoy all the benefits of their special status. Among them:

- If they make a bad business deal, the government bails them out.
- If they want to hire workers at below-market wage rates, the government provides the means to do so.
- If they want more time to pay their debts, the government gives them an extension.
- If they want immunity from certain laws, the government gives it.
- If they want to ignore rules their competitors must comply with, the government gives its approval.
- If they want to kill legislation that is intended for the public good, it gets killed.[15]

Today, the incursion of the United States into the Middle East is generating antagonisms similar to those manufactured to support World War II. This time, it is against Muslims. This war is not the choice of the American people. A few men at the top of the government took it upon themselves to wage war. It is an instance of egregious abuse of power flowing from male dominance at its worst.

Listen to some voices from History, from two very different speakers: Representative Abraham Lincoln in 1848, and Nazi Reichsmarshall Hermann Goering, imprisoned in Nuremberg in 1946:

Allow the President to invade a neighboring nation whenever *he* shall deem it necessary to repel an invasion, and you allow him to do so *whenever he may choose to say* he deems it necessary for such purpose—and you allow him to make war at pleasure...[16]

Why, of course, the people don't want war... But, after all, it is the leaders of the country who determine the policy and it is always a simple matter to drag the people along, whether it is a democracy or a fascist dictatorship or a Parliament or a Communist dictatorship. ...All you have to do is tell them they are being attacked and denounce the pacifists for lack of patriotism and exposing the country to danger. It works the same way in any country.[17]

In World War II, the United States' involvement was both an example of and an exception to Goering's comments. During the hostilities, demonization of the Germans and Japanese was extreme. But look what happened in victory: the United States became a major benefactor of both countries, contributing to a resurgence of their economies and the establishment of stable democracies. This illustrates both the evil that flows from inequality and the greater power of love to promote freedom and equality.

Impact of hierarchy on its members. The basic relationship consists of two people. In a hierarchy, the nature of their relationship depends on how they view the inequality between them. Because a fundamental principle of hierarchy is that an individual is more important than a relationship, in a hierarchical relationship, the person with more power believes his control of the other is legitimate. Inequality and control are the heart and soul of hierarchy.

The other person can resist being controlled and can compete, but obviously, in this situation, the higher-up has a competitive advantage. There is always a winner and a loser. The option to promote equality is never considered. Consequently, persons in higher positions are catered to and flattered by their subordinates, who hope to be rewarded.

From its members, the hierarchy expects or demands loyalty, productivity, cooperation, obedience, and self-sacrifice. A member is expected to support the organization's goals and objectives and accept the established system of rewards and punishments. And too often, an individual is important to the hierarchy only so long as he conforms and produces. Beyond this, he is disposable and is disposed of. Contracts are voided. Promises are broken. The former member becomes invisible or a threat to the hierarchy.

Individuals compete for higher positions in the hierarchy in order to achieve more equality and power, but this goal is an illusion. Each success presents another competition, even at the top. Inequality is constantly reinforced while the individual strives to replace those higher up or to not be replaced by those below.

As an individual climbs within the hierarchy, excessive abuses of power are prevented by competition. Necessary relationships also restrain the individual's reptilian impulses. However, when he reaches the top, a transformation occurs: he is alone, he has relationships only with people he controls, and the reptile breaks free.

Extending the principle that the individual is more

important than the relationship, *he becomes more important than the rest of the hierarchy.* As Louis XIV of sixteenth-century France famously declared, "I am the State!" Self-interest entirely replaces the organization's interest. The leadership changes into an elite focusing more and more on its own interests, and those at the top use their control or influence to gain special privileges and perquisites for themselves.

With regard to women, their general hierarchical position appears to have changed little or to be worse now than it was back when humans lived in bands. Women are unequal to men in most hierarchies and go unrecognized in some.

Women have had to acquiesce to hierarchy. They have recognized male dominance as "the way things are" but know intuitively that inequality is not God's way. Hierarchies are flawed because they are almost all male-dominated and fail to recognize that the male-female relationship is the most important relationship in civilization. It is the absolutely essential element in the existence of human society.

In the case of population growth, women did the work of childbearing and rearing, but they are still not equal partners in the sexual relationship. Because men's sexual behavior was governed by primitive impulses from the R-complex for thousands of years, they never explored what it would be like under the influence of the higher brain. Most men are unaware that greater satisfaction is available to them in an equal sexual relationship.

In governments, women hold few positions at the top. Many other positions are available to them, though not on a par with men. Women have done better in legal systems, and prospects for the future are good. Within the military, there is reluctant acceptance at best. The armed forces are still the macho expression of the male ego. As they were founded on the fact of male physical superiority, how can women truly belong?

In most religions, women are regarded as inferior to men and are excluded from membership in the clergy. Buddhism is an exception in which women enjoy full participation as congregants and clergy. In other religions, women's participation in ritual varies widely.

Education has been an area for women by default. Historically, much of the education of children was part of a woman's childrearing responsibilities. When educational systems developed in modern times, lucrative management opportunities attracted more men to the field. Teaching positions, however, are still filled mostly by women.

Women have found increasing opportunities in business and finance, but top positions are still limited. The greatest opportunities are in owning and operating a business. One thing highly prized and respected by men is ownership. Overall, while women are moving up within hierarchies, their progress is limited by men's unspoken worldwide belief in the divine pyramid: "Women just aren't supposed to be equal to men!"

Sometimes individual leaders come along who are able to promote freedom and equality within a hierarchy, but such anomalies are usually short-lived. When those individuals are gone, the inherent forces of hierarchy assert themselves to reestablish inequality and control. Witness the recent history of Hewlett-Packard, a corporation originally built on principles of freedom and equality that encouraged creativity to flourish. The company thrived as long as Bill Hewlett and Dave Packard were involved, but their successors did not share the same philosophy, and the company suffered conflicts and economic reversals after Hewlett and Packard were gone.

Because hierarchy exists on a foundation of inequality, it is not surprising that occupants of high positions engage in corrupt practices and enact a philosophy of greed. Recall the axiom of Lord Acton: "Power tends to corrupt, and absolute power corrupts absolutely!"

As civilization developed after the discovery of agriculture about 10 thousand years ago, hierarchies grew exponentially, affecting almost every organized human activity. They intruded into personal relationships, especially relationships in families. For society as a whole, the impact of hierarchy has been negative. Discrimination, caste systems, racism, and slavery are all promoted and supported by hierarchies today.

The behavior of a hierarchy and its controlling individuals is very predictable. In the absence of a constantly reinforced culture promoting freedom and equality in relationships, the system will move in the direction of increasing control and elitism—even when it began with the best of intentions.

After World War II, the newly formed United Nations made a brave attempt to promote freedom and equality throughout the world by adopting and promulgating the "Universal Declaration of Human Rights" in 1948 (see appendix 1).[18] It was a shining moment in the history of humanity. The document reads like the manifesto of the way of love. Humanity obviously knows the goal—but it doesn't know how to get there, and the path is not through the hierarchy that subsequently took over the UN.

Rather than establishing the huge Secretariat, it would have been better to establish task groups of governments with specific, limited objectives. This could have prevented the development of the UN's huge bureaucracy and inevitable appearance of vested interests in the status quo. It could have been a step toward the new society. Instead, we have the Security Council, which is not promoting freedom and equality but is rather maintaining inequality and control on a global scale.

When examined, hierarchies can clearly be seen to have a bad record, because the individuals who control them exploit inequality in relationships and enrich themselves, regardless of consideration of the common good. And always lurking in the shadows is the threat of physical force, used when needed to keep the system in order.

But isn't that what hierarchy is all about? The only limits to curb these excesses of self-gratification within a hierarchical system are through true power-sharing relationships such as those set forth in the Constitution of the United States. Alternatively, we can work to replace our hierarchical organizations through building the new society (see chapter eight).

Chapter 4

Inequality and Evil

Inequality is the root of all evils.
There is no evil among equals.

There are dual concepts of the creation of the universe. One deals with the physical dimension, and one deals with the spiritual dimension. These concepts coexist interdependently, and neither inequality nor evil appears in either one—but freedom and equality exist in both.

The physical concept is described by science, which deals with aspects of the physical universe that are "provable" and does not admit of the existence of God. Science does not deny God exists. It simply, as yet, does not have any proof. The spiritual concept is described by metaphysics, which deals with aspects of the spiritual world and is founded on a belief in the existence of God.

Science proposes the creation of the universe, the Big Bang, was a spontaneous appearance out of nothing. Metaphysics proposes the creation of the universe was an act of God because before the universe, there was only

God, an entity of infinite power and peace. Everything in God is in perfect balance. There is no time, no motion. Therefore, if God could be observed from beyond the universe, God would appear as nothing.

Science postulates the universe consisted initially of the elementary particles (quarks, leptons, and electrons) and energy making up everything in existence today. The particles were free-floating and unconnected in a void that inflated almost instantaneously to the dimensions of the observable universe. At this point, the universe was in chaos because there were no relationships. Then, the four fundamental physical forces—the weak force (radioactivity), the strong (nuclear) force, electromagnetism, and gravity—came into play. They impelled the elementary particles to make connections, to form relationships, and the orderly evolution of the universe began.

Metaphysics postulates God created a void within itself, in which the universe could be created. Then, God filled the void with unconnected particles. These were free-floating and imbued with the qualities of freedom and equality. Although they were different, no particle was *better than* another and no particle *controlled* another. Next, God infused the universe with love—the ultimate power—and love ordained that relationships be formed on the basis of the freedom and equality possessed by each individual in the relationship.

Thus, inequality and its consequent evil, hierarchy, have no place in either concept of creation. They are products of free will, which came after humans appeared on Earth. The greatest problem in civilization today is inequality in personal relationships. And because all relationships are personal, the problem persists as a matter of individual choice.

In the purely physical, nonliving dimension of the universe, there is no inequality or hierarchy. All of the nonliving physical relationships that compose the universe are equal. So too are the elements that make up those relationships. An atom of iron is as good as an atom of gold—different but equal. Inequality is only present in the spiritual dimension, where life exists. As previously noted, it is an essential condition of relationships among species in the food chain. There, it supports the individual's legitimate self-interest, needed for survival and procreation.

Eventually, however, the corruption of self-interest by men led to the development of hierarchy among humans, which then spread to touch every aspect of human activity—and to play a role in all human relationships. In support of hierarchy, men subsequently conceived a "mega myth," the divine pyramid (illustrated above). Almost all people in the world today believe in and act in accordance with this myth. Even many who do not believe in inequality nevertheless place themselves within the pyramid.

The basic tenet of this hierarchy is that the occupants at each level are superior to all below, giving them the right to control the behavior of all below. There is no specification of purpose to this control, and it is theoretically unlimited. This hierarchy sets forth a basic inequality in the relationship between men and women, which is most important, because all other inequalities flow from it.

The men who devised the pyramid placed God at the top. God is assumed to be male, and his power is not absolute. It is conditional because in certain circumstances, determined by men, God delegates his power to men, but never beyond them. There are variations to this hierarchy, which only men are permitted to make. The second level can be modified to suit almost any race, religion, or ethnicity that circumstances might require (see below). The power distribution among levels, however, does not vary.

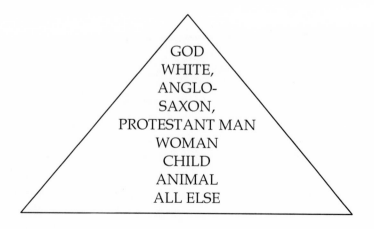

GOD
WHITE,
ANGLO-
SAXON,
PROTESTANT MAN
WOMAN
CHILD
ANIMAL
ALL ELSE

Another modification of the second level, as follows, is accepted throughout most of the world:

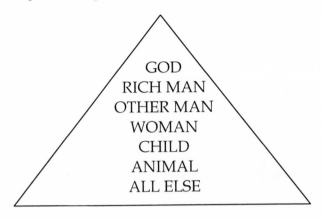

And even though the great spiritual leaders of history were poor and humble, you will never see this modification:

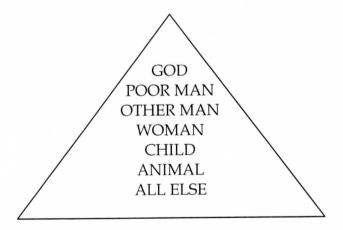

The important point here is that so many people believe this hierarchy to be legitimate—but it is false. God never ordained that relationships should be unequal.

If that were true, the physical dimension of the universe could not have evolved as it has. Unfortunately, worldwide belief in this mega myth supports inequality in personal relationships. And this leads to evil.

Evil is not some mysterious thing. Evil is any act that interferes with an individual's right to have relationships in accordance with God's divine ordinance. Evil is not a product of the Devil, much as we would like to shift the blame to such a creature. Nor is God responsible for evil. Evil is man's invention, and it does not exist outside of man. There is no evil in nature. Natural disasters are terrible, but they are not evil.

Evil is a product of human society. Each of us is capable of doing evil. Each of us is guilty of doing evil every time we support inequality in a relationship. Evil is a matter of choice. It is an exercise of free will. This means man is not controlled by evil and does not need to choose it.

During the last fifty years, many experimental demonstrations of discrimination and prejudice have been carried out, showing how behavioral abuses stem from beliefs in inequality. Three of these experiments stand out as particularly dramatic illustrations of situations in which evil ensued as the consequence of introduced inequality. In each case, all it took to create and sustain the evil was the input and approval of an authority figure.

The first example is psychologist Stanley Milgram's infamous 1961 experiment investigating obedience to authority:

The legal and philosophic aspects of obedience are

of enormous import, but they say very little about how most people behave in concrete situations. I set up a simple experiment at Yale University to test how much pain an ordinary citizen would inflict on another person simply because he was ordered to by an experimental scientist. Stark authority was pitted against the subjects' strongest moral imperatives against hurting others, and with the subjects' ears ringing with the screams of the victims, authority won more often than not. The extreme willingness of adults to go to almost any lengths on the command of an authority constitutes the major finding of the study and the fact most urgently demanding explanation.[1]

The second example took place during the two days after Martin Luther King, Jr., was killed in 1968. Teacher Jane Elliot conducted a demonstration of discrimination and prejudice in her classroom at the Community Elementary School in Riceville, Iowa. She divided the students into two groups, blue-eyed and brown-eyed. "On the first day, the blue-eyed children were told they were smarter, nicer, neater and better than those with brown eyes. Throughout the day, Elliot praised them and allowed them privileges such as taking a longer recess and being first in the lunch line. In contrast, the brown-eyed children had to wear collars around their necks and their performance and behavior were criticized and ridiculed by Elliot. On the second day, the roles were reversed and the blue-eyed children were made to feel inferior while the brown-eyes were designated the dominant group."[2]

What happened over the course of the exercise astonished both students and teacher. On both days, the group designated "inferior" took on the look and behavior of genuinely inferior students, performing poorly on tests and other work. Meanwhile, the "superior" students— who had been sweet and tolerant before the exercise— became mean-spirited and seemed to like discriminating against the inferior group. "I watched what had been marvelous, cooperative, wonderful, thoughtful children turn into nasty, vicious, discriminating little third-graders in a space of fifteen minutes," says Elliot.[3] She had created a microcosm of society in the classroom.

Elliot later observed, "I've learned that discrimination and its effects are the same no matter where you find them. I get the same results with the exercise in Berlin or in the Netherlands that I do in the U.S. or Australia or Curacao. And what's even more distressing is the fact that I've gotten the same results using the exercise with adults in Scotland and Australia in the year 2002 that I got using the exercise with children in Riceville, Iowa, in 1968."[4]

A few years later, the outcome of a "prison simulation" experiment was reported to the United States Congress by psychologist Philip Zimbardo, who demonstrated that even a mock prison is ruled by inequality and control, the essences of evil.

> What happens when you put good people in an evil place? Does humanity win over evil, or does evil triumph? These are some of the questions we posed in this dramatic simulation of prison life conducted in the summer of 1971 at Stanford University.[5]

Seventy young men responded to a newspaper ad for participants in a two-week study, during which they would live in a "prison" in the basement of the Stanford psychology building and play randomly assigned roles as "guards" or "prisoners" for $15.00 per day. The twenty-four volunteers deemed most psychologically stable and healthy were selected to participate. They were also predominantly white and middle class.

With the assistance of the Palo Alto police, the young men designated as prisoners were "arrested" at their homes, searched, handcuffed, booked at the station house, fingerprinted, and taken blindfolded to the mock prison. There they were stripped, deloused, given a uniform, assigned a number, and put in a cell with two other prisoners.

Before the arrests, an orientation session was held for the designated guards, who were told, "You can create in the prisoners a feeling of boredom, a sense of fear to some degree, you can create a notion of arbitrariness that their life is totally controlled by us, by the system, you, me, and they'll have no privacy... We're going to take away their individuality in various ways. In general, what all this leads to is a sense of powerlessness. That is, in this situation we'll have all the power and they'll have none."[6]

The conditions were aimed at promoting depersonalization and defeating individualism. The guards wore a uniform of khaki shirts and pants, along with mirrored sunglasses to prevent eye contact, and carried wooden batons. The prisoners wore uncomfortable, poorly fitting smocks and stocking caps, and a chain around their ankles emphasized their status as prisoners. Each prisoner's number, sewn on his uniform, was used by the guards instead of his name.

The first day of imprisonment was fairly

uneventful—then, the situation began to unravel. After only thirty-six hours, prisoner #8612 began to act crazy: screaming, cursing, and raging out of control. But it took the study administrators some time to become convinced he was really suffering and decide to release him.[7]

Prisoners received sadistic, humiliating treatment from the guards. This led to rebellion. A riot broke out on the second day, and the prisoners barricaded themselves in their cells. The guards, *without any administrators' instruction*, attacked and subdued the prisoners with fire extinguishers. They then resorted to tactics to divide them, which were largely effective: for example, designating a "good" cell block and a "bad" cell block caused the prisoners to suspect informers in their ranks.

Prisoners began to exhibit acute emotional disturbances. Disorganized thinking and crying were common. Two more prisoners had to be removed from the experiment early. The situation deteriorated further, and on the sixth day, after a visiting researcher found the prison's conditions to be appalling, the study was terminated ahead of schedule.

From a psychological perspective, the results indicated the situation, and not anything inherent in the participants' personalities, caused the behaviors. Zimbardo concluded, "After observing our simulated prison for only six days, we could understand how prisons dehumanize people, turning them into objects and instilling in them feelings of hopelessness. As for the guards, we realized how ordinary people could readily be transformed from the good Dr. Jekyll to the evil Mr. Hyde."[8]

As in Elliot's demonstration, the designation of an inferior group and its harassment by a superior group empowered by an authority figure resulted in dramatic, negative changes in the outlook and behavior of members of both groups. All three of these experimental examples give the lie to people, especially those in high places, who use inequality to commit evil acts and then attempt to justify such acts by saying, "Well, that's just the way life is!"

Inequality in relationships among living things grows out of natural differences in power, as it did with early man. It also depends on the perception of "separateness." The idea of male superiority—and female inferiority—originated in the bands during the hunter-gatherer period of human development. But otherwise, relationships in the bands were egalitarian. No one controlled the supply of food: each band member had equal access. There is even evidence of altruism in bands where a disabled individual was fed and supported by other members.

In Africa 70 thousand years ago, among all members of the small human population from whom we are all descended, there was very likely a sense of kinship. As mentioned earlier, kinship was important from the first appearance of life in determining relationships relative to the food chain, and kinship came to mean "like me." This basic form of recognition presented no problems when humans were concentrated in Africa. But after they migrated to all parts of the world, different groups evolved in very different ways. The concept of "like me" could no longer identify a common humanity as effectively as before.

The natural differences that appeared between groups have since been used to support inequality for millennia. *Different* has come to mean *unequal*, and today, inequality in relationships is "justified" by differences in age, religion, sex, material wealth, intelligence, ethnicity, politics, philosophy, and physical strength.

These difference-based inequalities did not exist in hunter-gatherer society. They appeared after the advent of agriculture, when food surpluses were produced for the first time in human history. Food became the currency of society. Control of food production and distribution created and sustained the earliest hierarchies of chiefdoms and states. With people staying in one place long enough to accumulate material possessions, differences in possessions came to determine social status and position. This bestowed power on wealthy individuals to determine the relative importance of other differences, such as religion or politics, in society's hierarchy. Does this sound familiar?

Control of wealth is so powerful because it controls the livelihood of individuals. Originally, wealth was food, and fundamentally it still is, as our civilization rests on the reliability and adequacy of our food supply.

The natural differences created by migration, agrarian civilization, and acquired wealth ought to be celebrated in relationships. However, some men exploited them to achieve dominance in society. This was a small step beyond the dominance they had exercised over women and other men in the hunter-gatherer bands, but with vastly more important consequences. It set up a sequence of conditions that degrades the quality of human relationships and leads to evil, as illustrated below.

Dominance
↗ ↘
Violence ↓ Inequality
↑ ↘ ↙ ↓
Resistance → **Evil** ← Separation
↑ ↗ ↖ ↓
Control ← Fear

Love, freedom, and equality do not appear in that diagrammed scenario, nor could they. Conversely, no condition in the diagram could exist along with love in a free and equal relationship. Rather, all of these conditions frustrate the need to love, producing some degree of anger.

- *Dominance* is the use of differences, real or imaginary, to establish a superior power position in a relationship. Dominance in and of itself is evil. It produces inequality.
- *Inequality* is an imbalance of power in a relationship. It leads to separation.
- *Separation* is the physical or emotional distancing of both parties in a relationship, due to an imbalance of power. It imposes limits and restrictions on interactions between them. Separation can arouse the primal fear of being alone (being alone was potentially fatal for early humans).
- *Fear* is the antithesis of love because it is divisive. It underlies all attempts at control.

Fear is the apprehension of loss or the belief that the partner in a relationship is dangerous and could be violent.

- *Control* is the exercise of power to influence or direct the behavior of the other person in a relationship.
- *Resistance* is the refusal to accept or comply with control. It is expressed through argument or actions taken in self-defense by a subordinate.
- *Violence* is behavior involving physical force intended to hurt, damage, or kill. It is the ultimate form of control and is an unacceptable way to resolve conflicts.

That sequence of conditions refers not only to relationships within and between hierarchies, but also to the most numerous and pervasive abuses in personal relationships. In the most important relationship in human society, the one between men and women, domestic violence is accepted worldwide. Proverbs of many nations present wife-beating as a "natural" and appropriate way to force women into subservience. The examples below reflect an obsessive male fear of being dominated by women. Men do not understand equality.

- To keep your wife on the rails, beat her; and if she goes off the rails, beat her.—*Spain*
- Beat your wife regularly. Even if you don't know why, she will.—*Sub-Saharan Arabia*
- Women and chops: the more you beat them, the better they'll be.—*Germany*
- Clubbing produces virtuous wives.—*China*

- Women, like gongs, should be beaten regularly.—*Korea*
- A woman who is beaten is going to be a better wife.—*England and the United States*
- The nails of a cart and the head of a woman: they work only when they are hit hard.—*India*
- For the man who beats his wife, God improves the food.—*Russia*

The extreme example of male dominance is rape. Rape is not about sexual gratification: it is about male control of the female. And yet, women can be punished for being raped! In India, they can even be killed!

All forms of violence are evil, from name-calling to pushing and shoving, slapping, spanking, physical assault, and assault with weapons. Martin Luther King, Jr., speaks eloquently of violence as "a descending spiral, begetting the very thing it seeks to destroy. Instead of diminishing evil, it multiplies it. Through violence you murder the hater, but you do not murder hate. In fact, violence merely increases hate. So it goes. Returning violence for violence multiplies violence, adding deeper darkness to a night already devoid of stars. Darkness cannot drive out darkness; only light can do that."[9]

In the second most important relationship in human society, between parent and child, inequality obviously begins at birth as a natural consequence of the child's dependence on his parent (s) for survival. It is subsequently reinforced by society's acceptance of inequality as the basis for all relationships. The child also has to accept whatever conditions he was born into. Hopefully, there will be enough love to soften the impacts of any abuses suffered at the hands of parents and other "grown-ups."

Even loving parents make mistakes: making negative judgments, being overly critical, violating boundaries, invalidating thoughts and feelings, shaming, and withholding or withdrawing love from the child. This sends a powerful message that love is conditional—not the unconditional gift God gave to us all. The most important contribution a parent can make to the life of a child is role modeling, educating the child to successful ways of living. If parents practice the way of love in their relationships with their children, the children will emulate them.

Where there has been abuse, individuals and society must then deal with its imprints. The negative effects of abuse and oppression persist for generations, even centuries. Where there is a history of slavery, the slave mentality of subservience and submission will last long beyond the life of the first one freed. It takes generations for a people formerly enslaved to understand what freedom is. It must be demonstrated by society as a whole, especially by people who *are* free, in their personal relationships with descendants of those who were not.

Billions of acts of abuse and oppression occur worldwide every day: in families, marriages, workplaces, governments, religions, schools, every human relationship where there is a hierarchy of power. That is the bad news. The good news is this is not what humans want.

The overwhelming majority of people want to live in peace and have stable relationships. Children play and go to school. Adults establish life partnerships, work, support their families, and pay their bills. Conflict and violence, although widespread, are not the norm—peaceful pursuits are. These include the peaceful struggle for equality, which will lead people to find the way of love.

Chapter 5

The Struggle for
Freedom and Equality

We have met the enemy and he is us.
—Pogo[1]

The struggle for freedom and equality in human relationships developed along with the evolution of hierarchy in human affairs. In fact, the struggle developed in response to hierarchy and its oppressions. This chapter traces the histories of hierarchies, their rise and fall, their abuses, and the struggles they brought into being.

During the hunter-gatherer period, humans fulfilled the self-interest aspect of the imperative to beget life by banding together for survival. All band members were committed to this common good and fulfilled the aspect of altruism by sharing food and by having and nurturing children. Men equated their own self-interest with the good of the band, employing all their senses to find food, protect the group, and father children.

There is no evidence of food hoarding or competition for food within the bands. But it was a sparse existence. For thousands of years, humans with our same senses and appetites enjoyed few rewards, never able to fully satisfy or overindulge those appetites. These conditions changed dramatically, however, with the advent of agriculture.

Between the development of speech 40 thousand years ago and the beginning of agriculture about 10 thousand years ago, some bands began to form tribes with hundreds of members. Around 10,000 BC, tribes of hunter-gatherers began to establish fixed settlements in a region called the Fertile Crescent, now occupied by Jordan, Israel, Lebanon, Syria, and Iraq. There, the tribes enjoyed a natural abundance of food, as fish, grain, fruits, and game were plentiful.

The settlements proliferated and grew into chiefdoms encompassing several thousand to tens of thousands of people, which created new problems of internal conflict. As Jared Diamond noted, these people "had to learn, for the first time in history, how to encounter strangers regularly without attempting to kill them."[2] The process of "liking" had to expand beyond kinship. It came to include all members of a tribe or chiefdom and finally, all those in the same ethnic, cultural, or governmental hierarchy (e.g., all Sumerians versus all Akkadians).

The advent of agriculture marked the beginning of a fundamental change in the way humans lived and related to each other. It allowed civilizations to develop. It supported human independence while, at the same time, it supported the development of the inequities of hierarchy based on the distribution of wealth. With only a few exceptions, the nomadic, hunter-gatherer lifestyle disappeared. Only after agriculture began to produce food surpluses, the earliest form of wealth, did humans begin to compete for dominance based on differences in wealth. Too often, this competition involved violent conflict.*

In the Fertile Crescent, Mesopotamia's most arable land lay between the Tigris and Euphrates rivers. There, the use of irrigation ditches enhanced production, creating surpluses and variations in the wealth of early farmers based on the fertility of their land. This led to the development of distinct social classes.

Before agriculture produced surpluses, men had competed within their bands for dominance and sex. Afterward, they competed within their settlements for food, sex, status, control, prestige, and material wealth. It did not take long for the characteristics of inequality, hierarchy, and violence to be expressed in—and between— the new societies. Food became the currency of the new civilization, and may well again.

Building on the success of agriculture in the Fertile Crescent, the area saw the rise of cities, the development of writing, and the creation of empires. In short, it was the birthplace of civilization and of the domination of human society by government hierarchies.

---

* Between 8000 and 5000 BC, agriculture's advancement enabled the establishment of communities such as Jericho, in 7000 BC "a thriving city of 2,000 to 3,000 inhabitants, a center of cultivation within a fertile oasis formed by the River Jordan."[3] But Jericho's construction as a walled fortress also evidences the lethal conflict among the humans in this region. Before agriculture, the greatest threats to human survival came from predatory animals. Since agriculture, greater threats to our survival have come from each other, especially from humans organized by a hierarchy to attack other humans. During the past 200 years, more than 200 million people were killed at the direction of dictators and governments![4]

Because food was the foundation of human society, for many years the chiefs of a state (or sometimes priests) controlled its production and distribution. Food surpluses supported the increasingly dense population in the Fertile Crescent and fed the chiefs, their retinues, and armies, and the nonfarming specialists who were essential to the further development of human civilization: craftsmen, merchants, priests, bureaucrats, tax collectors, artisans, and artists.

Although we can never fully know what occurred during the transition from the relatively peaceful, egalitarian band to the violent, hierarchical state, we can be certain of the evidence that this change took place over the course of millennia after the discovery of agriculture. One explanation of this process takes into account the enormous influence of our senses and appetites on the evolution of civilization. Some men may have realized they could have greater sensory enjoyment through controlling food and wealth—by force if necessary. Some achieved dominance over other men and women in the band. From later recorded evidence, we can infer that these dominant males, as protectors of the common good, probably had a key role in distribution of the food supply.

When farming produced a surplus, a chief knew how much he could keep and how much to give to his followers to maintain their support. He controlled the resources he needed to indulge all his desires. Individualism and hierarchy became the governing ethos of civilization. Chiefs also exercised a monopoly on the right to use force. They raised armies, became the permanent centralized authority, and made all significant decisions. Their positions were probably "elective" initially and later became hereditary.

Diamond eloquently described the worldwide evolution of hierarchy from band to tribe to chiefdom to state.[5] He also described the universal purposes of government: to pacify the people, by force if necessary (witness present-day Iraq), and to transfer wealth to the hierarchy's elite (witness the United States and third world countries).

An additional function of government is to bring into being or utilize existing religions to justify the positions of the elite and the transfer of wealth—the perpetuation and expansion of inequality and the limitation of freedom. These purposes and characteristics intensified after the transition from chiefdoms to states, which now control or govern all people on Earth.

It is significant that all of the attributes of modern society were displayed in the ancient civilization of Sumer, the first to develop written language and record its history. From this record, we can deduce that over thousands of years, human societies became increasingly productive, nonegalitarian, and violent. With a reliable food supply ensured and fixed settlements established, the threats to human survival were greatly diminished. This eroded the strength of the commitment to the common good, and the satisfaction of self-interest became the ethos of early civilization.

The Sumerians moved into Mesopotamia around 4000 BC and inhabited the region for the next two millennia, dominating Mesopotamian law, religion, literature, and science. Their greatest achievement, their system of writing, has enabled us to become very familiar with their civilization.

(The following account is based largely on C. Leonard

Woolley's *The Sumerians*[6] and Georges Roux's *Ancient Iraq.*[7])

A highly productive society, Sumer contained a number of cities and outlying areas. It undertook many public works such as road improvements, better canals for irrigation and water transport, and temples. There was great art and architecture. There was also inequality, hierarchy, and violence.

Inequality in relationships was expressed in many ways. The domination of women was codified into Sumerian law and later in the Code of Hammurabi. Women were completely under the control of their husbands or their husbands' relatives and had no legal recourse or protection.

The other dominated group in Sumer consisted of slaves taken in warfare. Initially, Sumerians justified taking slaves from other societies by saying their gods had made them victorious over an inferior people. Later, when wars between Sumer's cities were seen as wars between the cities' gods, Sumerians even rationalized making slaves of other Sumerians! (The wonderful neocortex at work! It also illustrates the selective nature of the expanded concept of "liking.")

Other inequalities are recorded in the Code of Hammurabi. The code sets forth an elaborate social structure: an upper class of "nobles" including government officials, priests, and warriors; a middle class of freemen who were merchants, artisans, professionals, and wealthy farmers; and a lower class of slaves. A citizen's rights and privileges were determined by his class. Punishments for crimes also varied according to the classes of perpetrator and victim. An offense by a perpetrator from a class lower than the victim's was punished much more severely than an offense against a social equal or a member of a lower class.

This society's religious hierarchy was dominated by an elite group of priests who ran a corporation that became Sumer's greatest landowner. The priests had once worked with others in the fields. Later, they hired the poor to do the work, claiming that their lands were really owned by the gods and that the workers' drudgery was required to support the leisure of the gods and their representatives on Earth.

At first, kings were elected by the commoners, but over time they became hereditary monarchs. They had the power to draft commoners for public works and levy taxes as a percentage of crops harvested. Most importantly, the monarch was a war leader and commanded the army. This was an important element of the state within a society where violence between major cities was common.

Perhaps the greatest monarch of Sumer was Sargon of Akkad. Between 2334 and 2279 BC, he created an empire extending from the Persian Gulf in the south, along the Tigris and Euphrates, to the Mediterranean Sea in the north. Sargon was a fulltime warrior and conqueror. His army numbered more than 5,000, and he kept it busy. After seizing all the cities of Sumer and leveling their walls, he turned to monopolizing trade. This was a key factor in his power, as was loot.

He especially prized human loot—slaves. Peoples vanquished in war became slaves to the victors, and Sargon and his sons acquired thousands. One son, Rimush, took 4,000 in one campaign. The accounts of slavery in Sumer are the earliest documentation of this evil.

Sargon's dynasty lasted more than a century, although the peoples he conquered often rebelled. His successor,

Rimush, was killed in a palace revolt and succeeded by his brother, Manistusu, who met the same fate. The empire lasted beyond the rule of Sargon's grandson, Naram-sin, until 2193 BC. After that, as a result of internal revolts and external invasions, it dissolved into anarchy.

Roux observed that this cycle epitomizes the region's history of hierarchical rule and conflict. "The rise and fall of the Akkadian empire offers a perfect preview of the rise and fall of all subsequent Mesopotamian empires: rapid expansion followed by ceaseless rebellions, palace revolutions, constant wars on the frontiers, and in the end, the *coup de grace* given by the highlanders: Guti now, Elamites, Kassites, Medes, or Persians tomorrow."[8] To this list we can add modern-day Shiites and Sunnis. It is perhaps not surprising that Iraq is still in chaos today.

Mesopotamian history, as the first documentation of civilization, describes the rise and fall of a society founded on inequality—an inequality based on differences in material wealth. It dramatically illustrates the human behaviors evoked by inequality: development of class distinctions, concentration of wealth, rule by a privileged elite, and interpersonal violence. This behavior pattern did not originate, however, with the Mesopotamians. It was probably established in the Fertile Crescent thousands of years before, shortly after agriculture's first surpluses. It was then amplified in later eras by surpluses in other forms of material wealth. The same behavior pattern has persisted over centuries to this day.

Since the time of Sargon, the dominance of hierarchy in human affairs has not really changed. Great spiritual leaders—Moses, Jesus, Mohammed, Buddha, Confucius, many others—have given solace and inspiration to billions of people, but their teachings have had little influence on the hierarchies of government, religion, and commerce. Even the disavowal of slavery was a victory of citizen activism rather than an acknowledgment and rejection of slavery's evil by the hierarchical elite in power.

Many other great civilizations such as those of Greece and Rome have come and gone, created and sustained by military conquest and then conquered in their turn. Historian Steven Muhlberger wrote:

> ...All empires are to a great degree pyramid schemes built on loot. A conqueror like Sargon gains followers with the promise of loot stolen from other people. Once victory is won, the benefits are quickly dispersed. Some must be reinvested in further war, which is waged in part by the people just conquered. Some must be distributed to deputies, generals and vassals. Only continuous conquest keeps the system moving, and even that is not sufficient: once paid off, vassals and officials start pursuing their own ambitions and become less biddable. Even the most successful conquerors, or their descendants, eventually reach one limit or another: the limit of successful campaigning, the limit of loot to buy loyalty, the limit of resources, which are being ground up in unproductive warfare. Somewhere the system breaks down, and some new group of thieves, unconquered barbarians or renegade imperial deputies starts carving out new kingdoms from the old.[9]

Thankfully, the arts and literature of great empires were preserved and have exerted a positive influence on society. Artists, in fact, have been the most effective counterbalance to hierarchies' oppression over the centuries.

The development of European and Western civilizations has seen the abandonment of the barbaric cruelties of the Middle Ages and the horrific practices of the Inquisition, but "lesser" forms of torture are still governmentally sanctioned, as are "cruel and unusual punishments." Governments are also still engaged in the transfer and concentration of wealth in the elite.

Ironically, these kinds of behaviors by "legitimate" authorities sustain the opposing struggle for freedom and equality. Commoners have historically believed in and supported the inequalities and limitations on freedom that hierarchies imposed—but there have been limits. Like waves, which crash when their height exceeds one-seventh of their base, excesses of the elite create resentments that break out in rebellions and revolutions when those excesses cross the thresholds of tolerance.

Unfortunately, as author Jeff Vail observed, "The downtrodden and oppressed of history have tended to fight hierarchy by organizing themselves into a semi-hierarchical structure. The problem with this process is that *if* they defeat their hierarchical opponent, the victorious downtrodden masses suddenly find that the traction of the hierarchical institutions introduced along the way to victory [has] too much inertia, and the new society eventually becomes just another oppressive hierarchy."[10]

In modern times, the American (1776), French (1789), and Russian (1918) revolutions are examples of one hierarchy's succession by another. The 1848 revolutions throughout Europe (in France, Austria, Hungary, the German and Italian states, and Poland) are examples of failed revolts. The overall goals were always the same—greater freedom and equality—but were limited to the relationship between citizens and government. There was no goal of replacing hierarchies with a new form of government. The revolutions were put down quickly, after terrible violence. Thousands were tortured and killed, and a decade later, not much had changed.

The struggle for freedom and equality in relationships began long ago in the chiefdoms, humanity's first form of stratified society. Chiefdoms were also the first societies to engage in slavery. Initially, slaves were used as manpower for menial tasks. When chiefdoms later developed into states, slaves were used in major public works such as irrigation systems, the great pyramids of Egypt, and the Great Wall of China.

Newly taken slaves were probably the first humans to articulate a desire for freedom. Having been freemen once, they could define freedom and equality as something that had been taken away. They may not have conceived of freedom and equality as God's divine gifts, but the urge to be free, to not accept slavery, came from within.

For thousands of years, the struggle was physical and political. Now, it is also spiritual. The urge to be free and equal is organic. I mentioned earlier that the cells of our bodies are composed of elementary particles existing since the moment of creation, endowed at that time with freedom and equality—so every particle of our being still contains those inherent qualities.

Inequality developed originally more by accident than

design, but it has been reinforced by free will as expressed through hierarchical leadership. The human impulse to be free and equal has therefore been suppressed for hundreds of thousands of years, but it cannot be denied. The expression of this impulse is also something that can be supported by free will, as exercised by choosing the way of love instead of domination.

The oldest organized struggles for freedom and equality were against hierarchies of government, religion, and commerce. Throughout human history, there has been a relentless struggle to increase individual freedom within hierarchies. Progress has been slow, but the struggle has had some success. Many dictators have been killed or expelled, many kings have yielded to parliaments, and governments of nation-states have been compelled to give citizens the vote. Religions' leaders have delegated power to clergy and congregations. Corporation heads have had to cede some control to shareholders and labor unions.

The struggle's success has been limited, however. Because hierarchies are founded on inequality and control, what begins as a struggle for equality within a hierarchy often becomes a struggle for superiority. In hierarchical terms, we call this ambition. Although it is commonly judged to be a good thing, too often it leads to corruption and evil. Achieving true, lasting freedom and equality within hierarchy is impossible.

Is this in conflict with the hope that it can be achieved in a democracy? No, because the hope is not that complete freedom and equality can be achieved in a democracy (witness the current inequalities in the United States). The hope is that democracy is the form of government with the greatest potential to be transformed into a free, equal society.

Future successes in individual struggles for freedom and equality will not come easily. We have been conditioned for thousands of years to support hierarchy and accept inequality. We have been taught to believe that obvious differences in ability or circumstance mean we cannot be equal in relationships—rather, that we are either *better than* or *not as good as* other individuals.

Equality is mostly seen in individual behavior and creative collaborations. Equality in relationships is too rarely seen and is not easily understood. It is not taught by parents, schools, governments, or religions. It does not mean equality in achievements: these are differences that can be celebrated. Basically, it is for each partner in a relationship to have an equal voice in matters of mutual interest. It may be that the power of decision has to rest with one person, but actions will not be unilateral.

As we strive to be free and equal in relationships, individuals will find the way of love for themselves, and their example will encourage others. It will spread, as did the domination of women by early man, when the example of some men was followed by others and became a worldwide ethic. The behavior of those early men was governed by their "old brain," which had not yet evolved beyond the struggle to survive. But all of us now possess the "higher brain," and there are enough of us whose lives are governed by it to make a beginning. We can make a difference.

Or, we can avoid the personal responsibility involved in eliminating inequality by saying, "Well, that's just the way life is! There's nothing I can do about it." But every day, in every interaction, in every relationship, we do have a choice: to promote freedom and equality, or inequality and control. Overall, freedom and equality means sharing power in all relationships.

Our lives are defined more by our relationships than our achievements. Our achievements are ours alone, but they do not define who we are. To focus on them exclusively is to be divisive and focus on inequalities. Just as our personal lives are best defined by our relationships, so is the life of humanity as a whole. Whatever our nationality, we feel good about the achievements of our society, but they also serve to divide us from other societies. They produce inequalities.

Aristotle said, "Everything in the world is moved by an inner urge to become something greater than it is." So it is with us. We have an innate but often subconscious desire to be free and equal in all areas of human activity: political, religious, economic, educational, and familial. These are very important relationships. And the most important relationship of all for survival of the species is the one between men and women, owing to the facts of procreation. In addition, when the relationship between a man and a woman is free and equal, their relationships with others tend to be the same.

There is no real basis for inequality between men and women. Neither can survive or succeed without the other. They have the power to correct the existing flaw in male-female relationships. They can mutually promote freedom and equality in their relationships as they understand the words. In this endeavor, men will have the greater difficulty in finding the way of love. They can say they are dominant, they can believe they are dominant, they can actually *be* dominant, but they do not seem very happy with the result.

I ask, "If male dominance is natural, why is it not accepted and celebrated by all women, children, and dominated males?" Instead, women get distant or mysterious. Children rebel. Men challenge other men. And when the sex lives of dominating males are unfulfilling, they turn to prostitution and pornography.

Actually, men have been deeply injured by male dominance. In an unequal relationship, both people suffer. Both are denied the comfort of the deep intimacy offered by unconditional love. Although men are reluctant to admit it, the apparent success achieved through dominance is deeply disturbing. Many men are also increasingly aware of, and uncomfortable with, the newly emerging ambiguity of their position in society. They support and defend male dominance, hierarchy, and inequality on the one hand while struggling to achieve personal freedom and equality on the other. This can lead to a very stressful internal conflict!

In advancing societies, men are questioning their traditional roles—this is the higher brain's altruism coming to the fore. Psychologist David Powell described the first half of most men's lives as a "journey of ascent,"

> ...climbing the corporate ladder and striving to excel in one's career, while focusing steadfastly on pursuing status and financial success. Somewhere in mid-life, however, most men are confronted with an inescapable feeling that their lives have fallen severely out of balance. Indeed, the price we pay in striving for success can exact a heavy toll in deflecting us from the joys and rewards associated with the *softer* side of life—the nurturing, caring relationships with our partners and children, and

having a positive impact on the lives of those around us, and just plain letting our hair down and having FUN![11]

Women, for their part, are actively striving to expand their roles. They are moving closer to their goal of equality, which they openly express. In contrast, men do not pursue that explicit goal, although they urgently need it. They see the changes in their relationships with women as a loss of power, not as a movement toward a more fulfilling life and a more desirable society.

The most important and challenging task for men will be to achieve equality in the sexual relationship. Because men have dominated women in sex from primeval times, they have not explored sex's potential in the context of a higher consciousness. Our sexual behavior is still dominated by the primitive part of our brain—very much like chimpanzees. A change in that behavior will only result from a conscious choice governed by the higher brain.

Evidence of the need for men and women to better understand their sexual relationships can be seen at any newsstand today. Article titles on the covers of popular magazines persistently illustrate our lack of success in two vital areas of human activity: weight loss and sex. We have a lot to learn. Men and women need to realize that their full potential depends on the establishment of freedom and equality in their relationship.

As civilization has advanced, power has been distributed more widely within hierarchies, but this was achieved mainly through violence and bloodshed. The problem with these battles is that they tend to be used as evidence of hierarchies' right to exist. In God's universe, there is no such right.

Over the last few centuries, many countries have established democracies, which appear to be the form of government providing the greatest political freedom and equality to their citizens. But they are new, and their success is still in question, because they are hierarchies nonetheless.

The appearance of equality in a hierarchy is a fragile thing. It is always hard won, and it can be taken away. The inherent forces of inequality are always arrayed against it. In 10 thousand years, the best example of equality within hierarchy we have produced is the United States. It is only 233 years old, and look at the prodigious efforts currently being made in this democracy to return to the law of the jungle! What politician today would have the courage of the signers of the Declaration of Independence to pledge "our Lives, our Fortunes and our sacred Honor"?

Abraham Lincoln understood the strength and fragility of democracy, attesting to both in his Gettysburg Address: "Our fathers brought forth...a new nation, conceived in liberty and dedicated to the proposition that all men are created equal. Now we are engaged in a great civil war, testing whether that nation or any nation so conceived and so dedicated can long endure."[12] Lincoln understood the fundamental nature of freedom and equality and the powers of inequality.

Once again, freedom and equality are under attack in the United States—this time, by the very men elected to protect both, who appear not to believe in either. Many members of the present administration and Congress are trying to reverse many years of progress made in civil liberties. Bill Moyers asserted, "Their stated and open aim is to change how America is governed—to strip from government all its functions except those that reward their rich and privileged benefactors."[13]

It is an ungodly crew such as history has seen time and time again. They support racism and are allied with the hierarchies of wealth, business, and some fundamentalist Christian churches—strange bedfellows indeed! They have no sense of God's relationship to humanity. It is frightening, but not surprising, that such men have reached the top of the government hierarchy. Hierarchy is inequality. Inequality leads to evil acts, which are the currency of evil men. At least we still have the power to remove them from office and try to repair the damage done by their evil.

The present struggle for freedom and equality will not be violent, though it may stimulate violent reaction. In 1976, author Marilyn Ferguson characterized this movement as "a different kind of revolution, with different revolutionaries. It looks to the turnabout in consciousness of a critical number of individuals, enough to bring about a renewal of society."[14] It will involve multitudes of people taking action to find the way of love best suited to their own lives. It will not need marches or parades. It may involve informal networks or small groups sharing their experiences.

The Internet will be a marvelous resource in this regard. Long before the Internet's widespread public use, Ferguson wrote, "Anyone who discovers the rapid proliferation of networks and understands their strength can see the impetus for worldwide transformation. The network is the institution of our time: an open system, a dissipative structure so richly coherent that it is in constant flux, poised for reordering, capable of endless transformation."[15]

Larger-scale actions against evil will continue, but these will be peripheral to personal struggles. The challenge for individuals will be in finding pathways for personal transformation. There will not be any collective action against hierarchies. Instead, the focus will be on promoting freedom and equality in personal relationships outside of hierarchies: in families, between husbands and wives or other life partners, between parents and children, among siblings, and in friendships. Too often, these relationships have been contaminated by a spillover of inequality from hierarchical relationships. But they offer the greatest opportunities to find the way of love.

We can replace the dominance of hierarchy with a new society devoted to the enhancement of the common good. It will be difficult. It means making the relationship more important than the individuals involved. It means educating rather than teaching; collaborating rather than directing; and most importantly, talking without fear.

In an unequal relationship, freedom of expression suffers most. It is replaced by fear. A child is afraid of being scolded or criticized. A student is afraid of looking stupid. Husbands and wives are afraid of arguments. A worker fears his boss's opinion. And many people worldwide are afraid of arrest, imprisonment, or worse, simply for talking. As individuals, we can change all that. We can replace the fear in relationships with freedom and equality—with love.

Chapter 6

Separation

The importance of separation is that it must be overcome.

The operation of the universe involves an endless creative process, an alternation between two phases in the evolution of matter and life: separation and combination. There is no choice in this. Everything in the universe, from particle to person, is involved in the process.*

Your life is an example. Your appearance in the world was a separation event, as birth separated you from your mother. Your conception was a combination event, when a sperm and an egg entered into a lifelong relationship.*

---

* Psychiatrist Gregory Fricchione characterized the separation/attachment dialectic as the tension between individuation and connectedness in human development. He defined altruism as "the healthy synthesis of self-affirming/self-realizing love (that which separates us out as individuals) with self-giving love (that which attaches us in empathy to community."[1]

* This is a good illustration of how a relationship based on freedom and equality is formed between entities that are different.

They produced an embryo that could become a human being.

These two phases, separation and combination, together define the evolutionary cycle, which seems to be one purpose of creation. The cycle began the moment the universe was created and is repeated endlessly in both the physical and spiritual dimensions. Although we do not understand why, another purpose of evolution seems to be to produce, through relationships, entities of ever-increasing diversity and complexity.

First came the separation phase. As discussed previously, God and the Big Bang produced the fundamental particles as independent entities. They were free and unconnected, different but equal. By themselves, the particles amounted to nothing but "quark soup." Then came the combination phase, conceived to overcome separation. God infused love, including the four fundamental physical forces, into the universe, and the particles were impelled to form relationships.

Although the evolutionary cycle consists of those two phases, the combination or relationship phase appears to be more important for humans. Unlike nonliving substances and other animals, humans are required to make conscious choices to overcome separation. They must resist powerful internal and external forces urging them to choose individualism over relationship, independence over collaboration. It is necessary to use the highest abilities of our brain to triumph over these forces. But we can do it because we are free.

In the physical dimension, the evolutionary process for nonliving matter is a development from the simple to the complex. It has not changed over the whole of the universe's existence. New entities and new relationships arise from combinations of old ones. From particles come atoms, elements, molecules, compounds, planets, stars, and galaxies. All of these relationships are formed by entities possessing freedom and equality. If the particles did not have these qualities, the universe could have ended up as a colossal lump of iron or a mass of gas like Jupiter.

The process is straightforward. When the entities involved join together, they produce new entities with properties not seen when they are separate.* This suggests science has not yet discovered all the powers particles possess. For example, we do not yet understand how particles produce different elements by forming different relationships with each other—just as we know a single human cell can develop into a complete human being, but we do not know how it happens.[2]

The important points about evolution in the physical dimension are

1. In the alternation between separation and connection, the physical entities involved are not changed by the process.
2. Physical entities do not possess self-interest.
3. Relationships are basically additive: that is, they produce something more than existed before the physical entities were joined.
4. The physical entities involved contribute to the formation of their environment but do not actively interact with or change their environment.

---

* Water's components, hydrogen and oxygen, are both gasses in their natural state. However, the natural state of their compound, water, can be solid (ice), liquid, or gas (vapor).

In the spiritual dimension, however, the evolutionary process is quite different, as follows:

1. Spiritual relationships are superimposed on physical relationships.
2. Life forms are changed in the process of alternating separation/connection by the requirements of feeding and eating.
3. Relationships are transformative: that is, life forms are involved in continuous change from simpler to more complex.
4. Life forms interact with and change their environments.
5. Humans surpass all other life forms in the ability to not only adapt to almost any environment but also to modify environments to better support and enhance their lifestyles.

When life appeared, a fundamental change occurred in the nature of relationships due to the simultaneous appearance of the food chain (see chapter one). Separateness and self-interest emerged as important considerations in the relationships of all living things. Control, inequality, and fear emerged in the predator-prey relationship. Living organisms, except for plants, had to choose what other organisms they would eat. The choices were unlimited until the development of mammals, the mammalian brain's prohibition against eating one's own kind, and the process of "liking."

Liking served mammals well for more than 100 million years. A great diversity of species flourished, especially during the past 70 million years, which included the appearance of our hominid ancestors. Liking worked best in small groups such as the bands in which our forebears lived for 2 million years. Remember that around 70 thousand years ago, our ancestors numbered 2–10 thousand, all in Africa, and they had not yet developed language. This placed great importance on the ability to visually identify "like" humans. It was essential for survival and was probably critical in the formation of the egalitarian relationships in the bands.

Then, several factors combined to produce humans who were "not like me." Population growth, migrations, and language resulted in separation again, of individuals and groups. Separation, in turn, led to the development of people who differed in appearance, speech, and behavior. And even superficial differences became synonymous with inequality. If you were not like me, you had to be dangerous or inferior. The hierarchies of governments, religions, and commercial corporations have exploited these natural differences ever since, and have used them to demonize the members of competing hierarchies.

We continue to use the liking tests in our daily lives. When strangers meet in peaceful circumstances, if they pass the visual appearance test, they engage in verbal testing, trying to find commonalities that could be used to establish a like-me relationship. Where are you from? Where do you work? Who do you know? When strangers meet in hostile circumstances, as with street gangs, failure to pass the visual or verbal test can be lethal—"kiss or kill."

Evolution in the spiritual dimension eventually produced sexually distinct human beings: males and females. Separate physical identities induced psychological separation, the development of ego, sexual competition among men (including interpersonal violence), and male dominance over women. The inequality in the relationship with women led men to believe that they, as the dominant partners, were more important and *superior* to women.

But this perception of inequality between men and women was purely a presumption on the part of men. There was no biological or physiological support for it. It was merely a matter of belief. However, it is important to note this belief still exists and has been expanded to include the idea that one person in any relationship can be more important and *superior* to the other.

A basic problem with inequality is that it perpetuates the state of separation and the idea of superiority. This is in fundamental conflict with the principle established at creation that the universe should evolve through relationships formed on the basis of freedom and equality. In the physical dimension, inequality and control do not and cannot exist. In the spiritual dimension, they are conditions chosen by some people to enhance the achievement of their selfish goals. These are the same people who capitalize on the reptilian impulse to create hierarchy and use it to justify inequality among people and the concentration of wealth and power in themselves.

Inequality is the essence of hierarchy. It is a concept that says individualism (separateness) is more important than relationship. The concept has been the foundation of civilization for more than 10 thousand years and is a major barrier to the formation of free and equal relationships. After living under hierarchies for millennia, we will find it difficult to overcome our conditioning to inequality and separation. It pervades our family lives, religions, education systems, ethnicities, and nationalities.

We also have a strong biological urge to accept and

support the separation and inequality inherent in hierarchy because of the impulses from our reptilian brain, telling us to be selfish. This part of the brain is concerned only with the self-interest and survival of the individual. It knows nothing of relationship or altruism or concern for the common good.

For primitive humans, our five senses were essential to survival and were also sources of great pleasure. They supported the appetites for food and sex. Sight, smell, and hearing helped humans to detect and evade predators and find food. The pleasures of taste and touch also enabled them to satisfy life's imperative. Self-interest was served by eating, and having sex produced progeny. In all of this, it is important to realize that sensory experience is personal. No one can really share your sensory experiences: your enjoyment at hearing the Beatles or Beethoven, the taste of ice cream or pizza, the sight of a Hawaiian sunset, the smell of coffee or perfume, even the ecstasy of sex. You can share your experience with another person, but that person will have his own experience. You will be physically together but emotionally separate.

As civilization advanced through agriculture, physical threats to human survival diminished. The pleasurable aspect of the senses became more important. The commitment to the common good that characterized life in the bands was eroded by an increase in self-interest. The production of food surpluses and fixed abodes allowed humans to indulge their appetites as they *never could* during hundreds of thousands of years as nomads. Small wonder that people began to compete for material wealth! The senses are so powerful and personal that they can easily overwhelm any consideration of others. The rulers of hierarchies know this and spend billions of dollars promoting sensory pleasures and diversions—satisfaction at the cost of separation.

Especially when young, we are easily beguiled by our senses. But we need to grow beyond the captivations of youth. Until we are able to do that, we can share experiences but not know the joy of intimacy that comes with equality.

Beyond the seductions of the senses, there is another challenge to forming free and equal relationships: the time it takes for a human to grow into a mature adult, which can be from twenty to thirty-five years. Growing up is difficult at best, and more so in any society burdened with inequality. Maturing involves the development of relationship abilities such as bonding, sharing, coupling, caring, and committing. These are ways through which we fulfill our most basic need: the need for someone else.

As we mature and experience different relationships, we go through five stages of psychological growth (characterized by psychiatrists Arthur B. Hardy, Clifford Anderson, and others). For the baby in the womb, there is no awareness of the existence of another person, and an infant up to about three months attaches to his mother with a sense of oneness. This is the most primitive type of relationship.[3]

As the child grows older, he recognizes there is a person outside himself on whom he is dependent for care. If the care is not nurturing, this relationship can produce shame and guilt that can last a lifetime—or, the child may grasp that because those he depends on have power over him, the most important aspiration is power over people. (And a way to have power is to have money.) On the other hand, if the care is considerate, he can develop trust and enter into a comfortable relationship of dependency.

Around age twelve or thirteen, he moves into adolescence and begins to develop a sense of identity by relating to and emulating people whom he sees as attractive models. He enters a period of independence often supported by rebelliousness. Around age twenty, the adolescent enters a period of interdependence and experimentation, which psychologist Kenneth Keniston referred to as "youth."[4] During this period, the young adult recognizes that others have needs in a relationship and struggles to find ways to accommodate them and his own.

It is a time of trial and error, when many errors occur in marriages, parenting, and other relationships. While the previous stages of relationships—oneness, dependence, and independence—are characterized by primary self-interest and immaturity, youth is the transition stage between immaturity and maturity, between separation and combination, and between self-interest and common interest.

It may seem late in life to start focusing on freedom and equality, but this stage offers the best opportunity to begin the transition to the way of love. Young couples are searching for intimacy. Young parents can begin to educate their children about the importance of relationships. Children may not be able to appreciate the concepts of freedom, equality, and the way of love until late adolescence, but they will emulate their parents' behavior. This can enable the new generation to find the way of love earlier in life.

The final stage of maturity is adulthood. The individual has developed the ability to commit and relate to others in mutually beneficial and fulfilling ways. He becomes less uncomfortable with uncertainty. Pure self-interest diminishes along with the desire to control others. Collaboration and partnership become the norms. Altruism becomes an important part of his lifestyle.

Obviously, not everyone achieves this level of maturity. Perhaps this is because the natural pressure from the senses to maximize the satisfaction of selfish desires is constantly reinforced by inequalities impacting us from the hierarchies in which we live.

One such impact has been the corruption of the concept of freedom. The time-honored definition emphasizes civil liberties, political participation, and social justice. It was included in the founding principles of the world's leading democracy, the United States. As sociologist Orlando Patterson described, "It is the version formally extolled by the [United States] government, debated by philosophers, and taught in schools; it still informs the American judicial system. And it is the version most treasured by foreigners who struggle for freedom in their own countries."[5] But now, for most ordinary Americans,

> Freedom has been radically privatized. Its most striking feature is what is left out: politics, civic participation and the celebration of traditional rights, for instance. Freedom is largely a personal matter having to do with relations with others and success in the world.
>
> Freedom, in this conception, means doing what one wants and getting one's way. It is measured in terms of one's independence and

autonomy, on the one hand, and one's influence and power, on the other.[6]

We have seen this version extolled at the top echelons of government. It is a current-day expression of reptilian self-interest. It allows for competition within a hierarchy with no holds barred. It can be used to justify any and all excesses in the accumulation of wealth. It is used to excuse any and all abuses, deprivations, and degradations caused by the concentration of wealth. It relieves the rich and powerful (or anyone else who can get away with it) of responsibility for evil. This concept of freedom separates the rich and powerful from the rest of society. It validates hierarchy and intensifies inequality. It glorifies the man at the top who was the "last man standing." If he has power, it does not matter how he uses it. His success is the epitome of individualism.

In the several stages of the process that produces evil (see chapter four), separation is produced by inequality and, in turn, engenders fear. The superior may fear loss of position, power, prestige, or possessions: "Uneasy lies the head that wears a crown." The subordinate may fear domination, control, punishment, or loss of livelihood.

The antidote to separation and fear is love—connection with another human. Like the inanimate elements in the universe, we respond naturally to the bonding power of love. But for the elements, it is a "straightforward" response, whereas for us, it is more "complicated." We must make an effort to connect and to stay connected.

In a recent study at UCLA, researchers reported, "It is already known that a person's social environment can affect his or her health, with those who are socially isolated—that is, lonely—suffering from higher mortality than people who are not. The findings suggest that feelings of social isolation are linked to alterations in the activity of genes that drive inflammation, the first response of the immune system. [They] found that what counts at the level of gene expression is not how many people you know, it's how many people you feel really close to over time."[7]

Separation has other consequences. It produces pain where previously there was connection: in divorce, death, and all meaningful goodbyes. When humans lived in bands, separation or banishment was a death sentence. Today, separation is invoked as a punishment throughout human society. The exasperated mother says, "Go to your room." The angry spouse invokes "the silent treatment." Nations break diplomatic relations with other nations. A government creates apartheid. A criminal is sentenced to prison, and in prison he is sent to solitary confinement.

Separation and separateness are major influences in our lives. Within hierarchies, they become instruments of control. But there is an important positive aspect to our separateness: we have the power to change. As individual humans, we own the divine gifts of love, freedom, equality, free will, and consciousness. These empower us to find the way of love—no matter that the rulers of hierarchies have corrupted the meaning of those gifts to support their own self-interest.

When a new issue arises in a relationship, the selfish reaction is "my interests." Question: Why shouldn't my wants come first? Answer: Because that can lead to evil, to the impairment of the relationship. The mature response is "our interests." It is not easy to overcome separation and to be loving, but attempts to maintain separateness and to be loving at the same time must fail. Between a man and a woman, this can produce a struggle for control of the relationship.

We are separate and yet connected. Each of us is a physically separate being from the moment of our birth. At the same time, through our relationships, we are emotionally and spiritually connected to the universe, the world, and the people around us. "We are caught in an inescapable web of mutuality, tied in a single garment of destiny. Whatever affects one directly, affects all indirectly."[8] We are not alone!

Relationships are the most important elements of our lives. To them we bring our personal feelings, desires, and messages from our senses to be melded with the feelings, desires, and sensory messages of another person. This is not a simple process, but the way of love can make it easier. When we promote freedom and equality in a relationship, differences between the individuals become unimportant. It is when we try to deal with our feelings, desires, and sensory messages outside of relationships, by ourselves, that we can be overwhelmed by negative emotions such as anger and fear, or beguiled by addictions and obsessions.

But we *are* in relationships, and through them we can resist the messages from our primitive brain telling us we are independent. As Carl Sagan asserted, "Neuroanatomy, political history, and introspection all offer evidence that human beings are quite capable of resisting the urge to surrender to every impulse of the reptilian brain."[9] The most important contribution we can make to the evolution of the universe is to promote freedom and equality in all our relationships. This is the way of love. We all need to find it for ourselves.

Chapter 7

The Way of Love

The way of love is of God.

The way of love empowers the evolution of the universe. It intends for all relationships to be formed on the basis of freedom and equality. It changes the universe. For us as humans, it is the purpose of our lives. It is for us to promote freedom and equality in all our relationships. Through us, the way of love changes civilizations.

But the way of love is a challenge to our free will, for it must be chosen. We must choose the quality of our relationships. They define our lives more than our achievements. It is only through our relationships that we can find the way of love. Our achievements are for others to judge and celebrate, but our achievements are ours alone, so to focus on them is to be divisive, for they cannot be shared.

The creation of the universe permitted our existence separate from its creator. That is the fundamental separation we are trying to overcome through our connections with each other. In the course of making connections, humans invented hierarchies, not realizing this was a colossal mistake. In early hierarchies and many that followed, the governing elites, sensing humanity's deepest desire, claimed they were closer to God than the common people were. Thus, they justified creating an imbalance of power and controlling the lives of others. In the final analysis, such an imbalance can only be sustained by the use or threat of physical force, and it denies the greatest power in the universe is love, which is the continuing presence of God.

Seeking the way of love results in a spiritual awakening, and it changes the balance of power in relationships. Hierarchies put power in the hands of the few, where it leads to corruption and abuse. The way of love affirms that the power of love belongs to every person on Earth. It is freely and equally available to each of us, every moment, every day. Only individuals can practice the way of love, and its power cannot be abused. The way of love does not supplant any belief system. Rather, it provides underlying support for all belief systems—just as a belief in inequality provides underlying support for all hierarchies.

Finding and practicing the way of love is comparable to playing music. All musicians accept a basic discipline, the musical scale, but each individual chooses his own way to express it, and the variety of expression is infinite. The challenge for the musician is how to express his music. The challenge for each of us is how to express freedom and equality in our relationships. Also in music, individuals can choose to perform together, to share their talents and expressions among themselves and with an audience. Similarly, when individuals find others with whom they can share their personal experiences with the way of love, they discover new, fulfilling aspects of their relationships.

The way of love is the path that leads us into a positive relationship with all people and our environment. No matter how unloving our feelings or actions have been in the past, we can seek the way of love for ourselves starting now. No one can be denied this opportunity, as it is the way of the universe. There is a constant opportunity to change relationships for the better.

To seek the way of love is a profoundly personal, spiritual quest. We cannot shift this responsibility to a rabbi, priest, monk, or ayatollah. Talking about our quest with others can be helpful, but we do not need anyone to guide us or tell us the way. The way of love is immune to the development of dogma, because it is unique to every individual. We cannot let others make choices for us: that leads inevitably to shame, and there is neither shame nor guilt in the way of love.

We have an inborn understanding of the attributes of freedom and equality. They are of our essence. Promoting them in all our relationships is the way of love—we need no further definition for our quest. To find the way of love is an experience of the moment. We will know every time we find it, because the feeling of fulfillment is unmistakable. And each time we succeed in finding it, it increases our ability to succeed again, until our quest becomes a constant companion of our consciousness.

In finding the way of love, there is no once-and-for-all. We cannot build up credits. The way of love consists of momentary connections. It is like breathing. Breathing supports our life, but each breath is separate and complete. We cannot take extra breaths today and skip breaths tomorrow.

We may never achieve a pattern of living in the way of love that is as natural and continuous as breathing, and no one will be able to practice the way of love all the time. Our goal is progress, not perfection. When we meet resistance, we let go, confident another opportunity will appear. As we develop our ability to make the best choices for our lives through our relationships, we will experience more and more moments of joy and satisfaction. And when many people have chosen to seek the way of love, its effect on hierarchy will be the same as throwing water on the Wicked Witch of the West—it will dissolve into the nothing from which it came.

The way of love produces mutual satisfaction in a relationship, because it is a way of giving and receiving at the same time. When I promote your freedom and equality, I promote my own. I do not need to make any judgments about you. My practicing the way of love does not depend on you. It has only to do with my expression of love.

The imperative for all things to love came as an essential element of creation. For nonliving entities, "love" simply meant "connect." When life forms appeared, love also meant to beget life—to connect and reproduce. When mammals appeared, love took on the added imperative to nurture the young. For people, love means showing concern and care for others, even at a cost to oneself. This is altruism, to which each of us owes our existence. It is inherent in human life. As expressed by philosopher Pierre Teilhard de Chardin, "Love alone can unite living beings so as to complete and fulfill them…for it alone joins them by what is deepest in themselves."[1]

In the life of early humans in Africa, there was no survival advantage in having a child. In fact, it was dangerous. Loss of mobility during pregnancy put the woman at risk from predators, and the man was at risk while protecting her. These risks increased after childbirth, with the additional burden of nursing and then sharing food with the child. The success of childrearing despite those obstacles is evidenced by the phenomenal growth in the human population since that time. It is the best evidence of the operation of altruism among humans.

Nancy Morrison and Sally Severino defined altruism in individuals as "a regard for or devotion to the interest of others with whom we are interrelated and with whom we express valuing of one another—including us—based in love.…Altruism is a dimension of spirituality that appears with the psychological changes in consciousness and self that permit the realization that we are all part of humanity."[2]

The meaning of "others" to whom altruism applies is thus extended beyond the definition of kinship as "like me" to include the whole of humanity. That spiritual and psychological development is supported by our biological inheritance, as detailed in the scientific literature. The prefrontal lobe of the neocortex enables us to form pleasurable attachments and avoid painful separations. Some scientists believe this ability expresses the separation/attachment dialectic from which altruism derives.

Regarding relationships within and among groups, the egalitarianism of the bands in the Paleolithic era (200–10 thousand years ago) had a profound effect on the evolution of altruism. Anthropologist Christopher Boehm posited,

The most radical effect of the egalitarian syndrome on human behavioral dispositions came in the social field, because of robust selection of genes for altruism. That evolutionary saga ends with a species altruistic enough to cooperate quite efficiently in large or small groups, but at the same time prone to competition and conflict. This cooperation is possible because human groups invariably act as *moral* communities that implement pro-social blueprints even as they suppress the aggressive egoism and dedicated nepotism that are so powerful in our nature.[3]

Boehm characterized human nature as rife with contradiction, "leading to…the ambivalence of our well-known selfishness and our long-denied altruism."[4] These reflect the dual aspects of the imperative to beget life.

Egotism and nepotism have been demonstrated continuously throughout recorded history, beginning with Sumer more than 5,000 years ago. Increasingly, however, our altruistic behavior is overtaking them—or, as Carl Sagan put it, "the gradual (and certainly incomplete) dominance of brains over genes."[5] This allows us to express our innate spirituality, choose the way we want to live, and become more altruistic. Our individual choices will affect others and produce a culture focused on the growth of the entire world community.

As expressed by His Holiness the Dalai Lama, "The central question—central for the survival and well-being of our world—is how can we make the wonderful developments of science into something that offers altruistic and compassionate service for the needs of humanity and the other sentient beings with whom we share this earth?"[6]

Accomplishment of that goal will be the product of a new society in which altruism and concern for the common good are the basic worldwide ethic. The focus will be on relationships, not individuals.

Questioning the foundations of individualism, the 2002 report of the President's Council on Bioethics rejects the idea that our worth is determined by what we say and do: rather, it endorses the idea that our worth is in our bodies and our relationships.[7] It also shows how far social thinking has moved in the past thirty years.

As noted by columnist David Brooks, "A generation ago, all the emphasis was on rebelling against conformity, on liberating the individual. Now the emphasis is on nurturing bonds so sacred they are beyond the realm of choice. Now the individual is less likely to be the fundamental unit of society. Instead, it's the family. In a mobile, high-tech age, the [council's] report is a declaration of dependence."[8] It portends a transition from a competitive, individualistic society to one which is empathetic and altruistic.

The way of love will have an impact on society through the important tasks we are to perform as individuals, since the opportunity and responsibility to find the way of love belong to everyone, regardless of differing circumstances. This means changing the character of our relationships from inequality to equality. This could be the most important transition of our lives. It might also be the most difficult.

As we focus on freedom and equality, we will see how pervasive control and inequality are in human affairs: they are the norm. To be successful, we will need to be persistent. Change will come slowly at first. Do not be discouraged. In our persistence, we may be helped by the Serenity Prayer of theologian Reinhold Niebuhr: "God, grant me the serenity to accept the things I cannot change, courage to change the things I can, and the wisdom to know the difference."[9] Remember, evil and inequality are man's inventions. Freedom and equality are divine gifts.

As we seek the way of love, we will also need to make many choices. Where do we begin this lifelong quest? To prepare ourselves, it can help to spend some time thinking about what it will mean to *us* to be free and equal. Our quest requires us to adopt what may be a new belief in equality and in our own value, both individually and within relationships. We will need to sustain this outlook in the face of society's current belief in inequality, while still living in our hierarchical society. How will we do it? What changes are important to work on first? What are the most important relationships to focus on? We cannot deal with all of them at once. It is important in the beginning to work on one relationship at a time. Go slowly. This is going to be a growth experience.

If possible, family relationships are a good place to begin. Families are so important in human society. They are the greatest opportunity for members of a group to establish free and equal relationships with all other members. It is truly tragic that this result is so seldom achieved even though family members possess all the power they need to achieve it.

Think of the emotional energy that could be saved and redirected if we were not concerned about familial judgment, criticism, or control. People who are free and equal in a relationship focus on collaboration, supporting and empowering each other. They produce something more, and usually better, than they could have produced acting separately.

As we assess any relationship (family, friend, or coworker), it is essential to remember that our part in the way of love is to *promote* freedom and equality—nothing more. That is our responsibility even when our partner does not reciprocate. We cannot impose freedom and equality on anyone, but we can be assertive and persist in our promotion.

"Nothing we do, however virtuous, can be accomplished alone; therefore we are saved by love."[10] So we need to focus on the relationship, not on the other person. Overall, do we feel positively or negatively about the relationship? Does it support us? Does it empower us? Does it diminish or demean us? Are we proud of the relationship? Do we feel guilty about it? And, most importantly, is the balance of power acceptable to us?

In a healthy relationship, there may not be a *precisely* equal balance of power—nor does there always need to be. And equality of circumstance may be impossible. The important thing is whether the power balance is meeting the needs of both people and moving toward equality. Any limitations on freedom and equality are defined by the conditions of the relationship.

Consider the special case of parenting: In the mother-child relationship, the mother has to hold most of the power, but not all. She also has to honor and encourage the child's power to learn independently, to walk, to talk, to play. As the growing and maturing child accrues greater power within the relationship, limitations will be increasingly determined by mutual consent, and the balance of power will move toward equality. All other unequal relationships could evolve in a similar way, once power is redefined as a means to an end and not an end unto itself.

An additional way to evaluate a relationship is to examine the motivations of our behavior. All of our behaviors stem from a motivation either inside or outside ourselves. For young children, motivations are largely external, because children are continually learning about living from their parents. However, motivations for some behaviors, such as walking and talking, are basically internal.

In our relationships, what is the balance between internal and external motivations? Is the balance appropriate for our life today? Is the balance evolving in a way that we like? Is the relationship improving or deteriorating? Is it healthy or unhealthy?

In all relationships, decisions and choices are made that affect both parties. In a healthy relationship, both parties are assertive and make their wishes known. If they disagree, they negotiate: "Let's flip a coin" or "This time you choose, next time I'll choose." In the way of love, agreements are often reached without need of negotiations. Partners will later say, "Whose idea was this anyway?"

But in unhealthy relationships, disagreements are characterized by conflict. One or both parties are aggressive, wanting or attempting to control the outcome, overriding all ideas but their own. Negotiation is not considered an option.

As we become comfortable with our practice of the way of love, our relationships will become stronger, deeper, more intimate and fulfilling. Trust will develop. We will have reached a truly significant milestone when we can talk to another person about our fears. We will change our thinking about power, seeing it as something to be shared.

We will discover a richer, more rewarding way of life that does not depend on possessions. Human relationships are spiritual, not material. They involve connections and an exchange of spiritual energy.

We do not have relationships with money or other material things, merely attachments—we own them, we have absolute control over them. To introduce material things into a relationship in any way other than to share them is to introduce inequality and evil into the relationship.

That very process, in fact, is fundamental to the development of a hierarchy. It is probably what happened after the advent of agriculture produced surpluses. When the individuals who controlled food production chose not to share food as the bands had, and instead offered food in exchange for something else, food became an element of control in society. The way of love cannot be found through wealth and power.

Because of the thousands of years humans have been conditioned to lives of inequality, our quest will be difficult. It means turning away from hierarchy. We will need to give up attempts to control others in our relationships, and we will need to trust in outcomes. We will need to become more comfortable with uncertainty, because we cannot predict from day to day what opportunities we will have to promote freedom and equality.

As mentioned earlier, the way of love is an experience of the moment. The rewards will be great: to be in control of our own lives, to experience the joy of relationships without conflict, to realize the full potential of collaborative effort, to experience a sense of peace not possible in a hierarchy.

As humans with free will, our relationships are

not one-time affairs. There is a constant flow of energy between people, and relationships do evolve. When there is increasing freedom and equality for both partners, their attachment to each other becomes deeper and stronger. This is the way of love, in which one person can act purely out of self-interest—that is, by choosing to practice the way of love—because that act is promoting the freedom and equality of another. The relationship becomes one of true sharing, in which giving and receiving occur simultaneously. Individuals are motivated to achieve their greatest potential. No energy is wasted on dealing with the stress involved in overcoming inequality.

In the way of love, power is shared by mutual consent. Problems arise when one person is dominating. That can lead to emotional or physical separation and fear, which is the opposite of love. Love is of God, fear is of man. When we are loving, we are open, close, and connected. We do not attempt to control anyone. When we are fearful, we are closed, distant, and separated, and we try to control other people. But we can choose the way we want to live our lives every day—loving and connected, or fearful and separated. As the most advanced species in the history of our planet, we have a choice in determining our present and our future.

During society's transition from an ethos of inequality to one of equality, we will need to deal with reality. We will continue to act against evil by being assertive (nonviolent) rather than aggressive (violent). And finding the way of love for ourselves will eventually prevail over inequality, because our quest is supported by the greatest power in the universe—love.

We have that power now. We can begin to change our life today. We have everything we need to find the way of love. We do not need to buy anything to find it. We do not need to own anything. We can learn from others, but we do not need anyone to teach us anything. We understand what freedom is, what equality is. As we promote them in our relationships, our understandings will grow and be transformed from "my" ideas into "our" ideas. That is the power of loving relationships. They produce something that did not exist before them. They transform peoples' lives.

Marilyn Ferguson described a transformative relationship in her remarkable book, *The Aquarian Conspiracy: Personal and Social Transformation in Our Time*, in 1976:

> It is a conspiracy of two, a momentarily polarized circuit of consciousness, an electrified linking of minds. It neither asks nor answers; it simply connects. It may be no more than a glance between strangers. And at its most complex and dynamic, it is the planet's brain, the accelerating awareness of brotherhood anticipated by Teilhard, Buber, Maslow, and others.
>
> The loving, transformative relationship is a compass to our potential. It frees, fulfills, awakens, empowers. You don't have to "work at it." With its curious blend of intensity, ease, and spiritual connection, the transformative relationship stands out in marked contrast to all the less-rewarding connections in our lives and becomes as vital as oxygen. Each such relationship is also a compass to another kind of society, a model of mutual enrichment that can be extended throughout the

fabric of our lives. The transformative relationship defines itself; it does not try to conform to what society says it should be but serves only the needs of the participants. There may be guiding principles, even flexible agreements, but no rules.[11]

Transformative relationships are at the heart of the way of love. We will find them as we dispose of the rubbish accumulated over our hierarchical history. We will be able to live more fully in the spiritual dimension. Evolution has been preparing us for this experience through brain development. The capabilities of our neocortex—which has been found to possess enormous unused capacity—make it possible for us to realize our full altruistic potential.

Men and women need to achieve sexual equality. Parents and children need to achieve greater understanding of each other. Leaders need to share power and relish accountability. Countries need to learn to be good neighbors (Canada and the United States are an existing "good neighbors" example). We all need to learn how to really share.

Participation in sports or the arts by anyone and everyone would be a great step toward a new society. Involvement in sports increases our awareness of the importance of cooperation and community. Involvement in any art form creates beauty for all to share, in painting, sculpture, music, dance, theater, poetry, or literature, and also transforms people's lives.

The way of love is not—and cannot be—prevented or controlled by any hierarchy. It is revolutionary. It is a nonviolent way to transform society that will not result from organized effort, but from millions upon millions of individual choices. The outcome of so many individuals seeking the way of love will be the creation of a new society in which freedom and equality will support all human activity. They will provide the context for greater success in any endeavor. To seek the way of love is to decide not to squander our precious time on Earth.

Decades ago, Sagan expressed the hope that "although we are still people from divergent cultural backgrounds, our intelligence is beckoning us toward greater webs of global relationship. In due course, we will simply be the 'whole human community,' the entire planet Earth. This process is already underway."[12] And indeed, hierarchies are quietly being replaced by networks. The Internet and the World Wide Web are accelerating this development. Power and decisionmaking are becoming more decentralized. Voluntary efforts are replacing all types of coercion. In the new society, the overriding goals of governments, businesses, and religions will be to recognize our common humanity and promote the common good.

Chapter 8

The New Society

You never change anything by fighting the existing reality. To change something, build a new model and make the existing model obsolete.
—Richard Buckminster "Bucky" Fuller[1]

To find the way of love—the purpose of our existence —is not a final achievement. It is not an end point. It is the beginning of a new way of living. It puts the power to shape the future in our own hands by establishing freedom and equality in relationships as the foundation of a new society. We can create that society. And though no one can say exactly what it will look like, we can make some predictions. The new society will be innovative. New social and economic values will be formed. For example, in Spain, the Mondragon Corporation exemplifies an innovative, even revolutionary economic concept based on the principle that all wealth is produced by workers. Therefore, ownership and control of the production and distribution of wealth is vested in workers. New ideas and products will flourish in what has been called "the fourth quadrant" (similar to the fourth sector).

Steven Johnson described the fourth quadrant in "Innovation: It Isn't a Matter of Left or Right":

> It is the space of collaborative, nonproprietary innovation, exemplified in recent years by the Internet and the Web, two groundbreaking innovations not owned by anyone. The Internet is the ultimate example of how fourth-quadrant innovation actually supports market developments: a platform built by a loosely affiliated group of public sector and university visionaries that has become one of the most powerful engines of wealth creation in modern times."[2]

Why has the fourth quadrant been so innovative, despite the lack of traditional economic rewards? The answer, I believe, has to do with the increased connectivity that comes from these open environments. Ideas are free to flow from mind to mind, and to be refined and modified without complex business deals or patent lawyers. This will characterize the new society. Furthermore, education will be universally available, since enlightened self-interest leads to healthy competition.

Like freedom and equality, creativity was part of the birth of the universe. Evolution is the grand creative process by which nonliving entities had the power to create distinct new entities, even life forms with creative powers of their own, which then joined the evolutionary process. Part of our cosmic inheritance, the seeds of creativity exist in all of us and may need only a stimulus to develop. For most of us, equality in relationships could be the impetus needed to produce a powerful wave of innovation and creative expression.

Creative expression has a transformative impact on the individuals involved and on their environment. During the past 10 thousand years, despite the restrictions imposed by hierarchies, creative individuals produced great civilizations and empires—e.g., Egypt, China, Greece, and Rome—which ultimately collapsed when the ruling hierarchies were unable to sustain them. In modern times, we have seen the rise of colonial empires and their fall after World War II: British, French, Belgian, Dutch, German, and Russian.

Interestingly, the artistic expressions of individuals from all these periods survived their governments' disasters, evidencing that the power of creativity is in people, not institutions. It is through creative individuals that important transformations occur.

At the end of World War II, the United States witnessed a dramatic illustration of the social impact of creativity. It resulted from millions of people choosing simultaneously to improve their lives. During the war, the ingenuity of Americans in the armed forces helped to shorten the length of the conflict. When millions of servicemen and women came home, they took advantage of educational benefits available under the GI Bill. Completing their schooling and applying their talents to all sections of the economy, they changed the face of the nation and influenced the world—creativity unleashed by education. So tremendous was their impact in war and peace that they came to be called "the greatest generation."

Examples also abound of how creative expression,

particularly through involvement in the arts, can transform lives at the personal level. In recent years, two documentary films have chronicled the personal transformations of amateur "actors" taking part in theatrical productions in unexpected settings: a medium-security prison and a troubled high school in a troubled urban community.

Every year since the mid-1990s, at the Luther Luckett Correctional Complex in La Grange, Kentucky, a program known as "Shakespeare Behind Bars" involves prisoners in one of William Shakespeare's plays. Guided by volunteer project director Curt Tofteland, inmates have performed dramas dealing with mercy and redemption such as *Othello*, *Titus Andronicus*, and *Hamlet*. In 2005, Tofteland decided to produce *The Tempest* and was joined by married filmmakers Hank Rogerson and Jilann Spitzmiller to make a documentary of the production.[3]

Casting was up to the prisoners, who chose roles touching on their personal stories. Individual histories blended with the play's plot, helping the actors to make searching examinations of their lives and crimes. When Hal, as the exile Prospero, recited, "O, what a cherubim thou wast" to the motherless daughter Miranda, he painfully recalled his terrible, murderous act that left his own daughter motherless. Red, playing the delicate girl, remembered questions about his own paternity that helped him to understand Miranda's questions about her mother. And Big G, to comprehend the brute Caliban, thought back to himself at twenty-one: a drug dealer who killed a policeman in a shootout.[4]

The resulting film, *Shakespeare Behind Bars*, is deeply moving (and the acting is surprisingly good). The program's therapeutic value is obvious. The film does not whitewash the acts that brought the men to Luckett, but it offers them dignity and a fresh look at the truth of their lives and the opportunity to change.

Southeast of Los Angeles, California, is the city of Compton, long plagued by street gangs fighting each other, some allied with Mexican drug cartels. Dominguez High School, one of three in Compton, embodies an explosive culture of black and Hispanic youths and was known for riots and ongoing gang violence. Students generally hated the school. Basketball was valued above all else, and there were proms, but there had not been a school play in more than twenty years. Then in 1998, English teacher Catherine Borek started a drama program at Dominguez.[5]

Aware of Compton's violent reputation and intrigued with Borek's plan, cinematographer Scott Hamilton Kennedy made several visits to her drama class. When he met the kids, many of the stereotypes he had harbored were overturned by their charm. When Borek and fellow teacher Karen Greene decided to put on a school play, Kennedy asked if he could film it.

Having no budget or stage for the production, Borek chose Thornton Wilder's *Our Town*, as it did not need costumes or a set and could be performed in the school cafeteria. Through the everyday lives of the people in a fictional New Hampshire town, the play explores timeless themes of love and loss, life and death, community, and family. At first, it was difficult for the students to relate to the material. What did Wilder's all-white town of Grover's Corners have to do with Compton? But Borek and Greene motivated the group to update the play and make it relevant to their friends and family.[6]

In the process of creating *OT: Our Town*, the students took a journey of self-discovery. They discovered the joy of transformation: the opportunity theater provides to become a character, go on stage, and show everyone what they are capable of. The resulting documentary demonstrated how art can break boundaries and teach us that the struggles we face are universal. *The Toronto Star* proclaimed, "Has there ever been a movie that shows more clearly how theatre can change people's lives? Marvelous!"[7] Since that production, school plays have been an annual event at Dominguez.

In both cases, the participating individuals changed their views of themselves and their place in the world. From positions of low self-esteem and antisocial attitudes, they came to believe they were worth something more. They aspired to make contributions to society, and felt they truly could.

Most people do want to earn their way in the world. Not merely a time-worn dictum of human society, "earning our way" has come to be recognized as an individual's right and responsibility. In the "Universal Declaration of Human Rights" proclaimed by the United Nations, articles 23 and 25 set forth our rights to work and earn a living adequate for the health and well-being of ourselves and our family (see appendix 1).[8] Unfortunately, the world's economic systems are not focused on the fulfillment of these rights.

In today's world, where almost everyone needs a livelihood, we have relationships based on economics. These reflect greater or lesser degrees of coercion, depending on the availability of alternative opportunities for individuals to earn a living. Consequently, we could characterize our civilization as a coercive society. We need a fundamental change to correct the evils of the past and to solve the problems of the future in a peaceful way.

The next forty years will present challenges the world has never faced. From 3 billion in 1950, we are now up to 6.5 billion. By 2050, the world population will number 9 billion.[9] That amounts to an increase of more than 60 million people each year! The pressure of this population on world resources will be unimaginable.

We also need to prepare for increasing globalization and the advent of a world community. Stimulated by the example of the American economy, many other nations are striving for comparable levels of production and consumption. According to one *Newsweek* report, "In 2006 and 2007, 124 countries grew their economies at over 4% a year."[10] These growth rates imply that the current level of consumption in the United States, with only 5 percent of the world's population, cannot be sustained in the face of increases in production and consumption by the other 95 percent. The production and distribution of wealth must, inevitably, become more equitable.

World governments, however, are inflexible. They are not preparing to enter into the cooperative relationships among nations that will be required to deal effectively with the major problems soon to be posed by population growth, environmental degradation's impact on the food supply, and globalization. In 1977, Carl Sagan pointed to hierarchy as the root of this inflexibility:

> In general, human societies are not innovative. They are hierarchical and ritualistic. Suggestions for change are greeted with suspicion: they imply an unpleasant future variation in ritual and hierarchy: an exchange of one set of rituals for

another or perhaps for a less structured society with fewer rituals. And yet, there are times when societies must change.

Much of the difficulty in attempting to restructure American and other societies arises from this resistance by groups with vested interests in the status quo. Significant change might require those who are now high in the hierarchy to move downward many steps. This seems to them undesirable and is resisted.[11]

At the time of Sagan's observation, the United States was a middle-class society, and the government's massive transfer of wealth to the elite had not begun. But by 1980, the top 1 percent held 20 percent of the nation's wealth. By 2000, they held 38 percent—a trend that accelerated under the Bush administration. The effect on the middle class has been devastating.

The wealthy and their associates in government and business have ignored Aristotle's ancient dictum of the perfect political community, "one in which the middle class is in control and outnumbers both of the other classes," as well as Plutarch's warning: "An imbalance between rich and poor is the oldest and most fatal ailment of all republics."

Similar gaps between rich and poor exist elsewhere around the world, some entrenched for centuries. In the United States, this march of folly began in the late 1960s. Sociologist Frank Furedi observed that conservatives were appalled by the "radicalism" of the decade, when "establishment values were ridiculed and rejected by a minority of young people. Cherished traditions were mocked and authority was questioned."[12] During the anti-war protests, President Richard Nixon actually felt we were close to a revolution. Furedi posited that the result was the creation of "the sixties myth"[13] and the construction of a conservative backlash.

The traditional forces of hierarchy reasserted themselves in the 1980s. With President Ronald Reagan, the wealthy elite accelerated their domination of society through the increasing concentration of wealth. With President George W. Bush, they added an attempt to create a one-party political system. These actions created wide divisions in American society and led to the alienation of the elite.

In *Collapse: How Societies Choose to Fail or Succeed*, Jared Diamond described the ultimate failure resulting from such a division:

> Wealthy people increasingly seek to insulate themselves from the rest of society, aspire to create their own separate virtual (enclaves), use their own money to buy services for themselves privately, and vote against taxes that would extend those amenities as public services to everyone else. Those private amenities include living inside gated walled communities, relying on private security guards rather than on the police, sending one's children to well-funded private schools, purchasing private health insurance or medical care, drinking bottled water instead of municipal water and (in Southern California) paying to drive on toll roads competing with jammed public freeways. Underlying such privatization is a misguided belief that the elite can remain unaffected by the problems of society around them: the attitude of those Greenland Norse chiefs who found that

they had merely bought themselves the privilege of being the last to starve.[14]

We need to find an alternative to these destructive patterns. We need to find the way of love, not just for our own sakes, but to reverse the direction in which the world is going, led by the United States. We need visionary thinkers urging us in a different direction toward the future, as Sagan further described:

> Unless we destroy ourselves utterly, the future belongs to those societies that, while not ignoring the reptilian and mammalian parts of our being, enable the characteristically human components of our nature to flourish; to those societies that encourage diversity rather than conformity; to those societies willing to invest resources in a variety of social, political, economic and cultural experiments, and prepared to sacrifice short term advantage for long term benefits; to those societies that treat new ideas as delicate, fragile and immensely valuable pathways to the future.[15]

The way of love engenders such a society. It would not be the result of any hierarchical endeavor—it would be the consequence of millions upon millions of people practicing the way of love. The transition from existing inegalitarian societies would be gradual and peaceful. And through the increasing interrelationships among different societies and cultures, the way of love would become the worldwide governing ethic.

The most important change in the new society would

be the achievement of equality in the relationship between men and women. With freedom and equality in relationships as its fundamental value, society's focus would shift from the man to the man-woman relationship and from the individual to the family—a *true* focus on family, not today's hypocritical "family values" hype. Benefits and liabilities would be shared, because a central characteristic of families is the sharing of resources. Society's structure would be transformed from relationships based on economics—which include most existing relationships (with the most extreme enslaving 27 million people worldwide)—to *economics based on relationships*, as we see in healthy families.

Because control and coercion do not exist between equals, human activity would be voluntary. Altruism would be regarded as a desirable quality to be emulated. The ethos of society would be the common good of families and communities. Organizations would exist as associations to serve a common purpose. Many would have only a limited existence and not be perpetuated to serve vested interests after their original purposes were achieved.

Adversarial relationships could be greatly diminished. Personal disagreements could be resolved at the personal level. Personal abuse could lessen. The purposes of a relationship would be the mutual enhancement of each partner's potential or a creative collaboration (such as Rodgers and Hammerstein, or Hewlett and Packard).

Differences in wealth could exist when society, through peer judgments, placed a higher value on an individual's contributions to the common good. But society would not value the divisive accumulation or concentration of wealth resulting from unrestrained competition or government transfers. Commercial competition could be about improving product or performance to benefit all, not about producing maximum profit for the few. (In athletics, competition could be to improve on personal bests—that would be experienced as reward.)

Children would be highly valued by everyone. Parenting could be seen as the great gift it is. Society would be permeated with an appreciation of the flow of life from generation to generation. A loving, lifelong relationship between parents and children could be considered the most rewarding personal achievement.

The new society would not turn away from the advances civilization has made. But it would be selective in what was kept—not those things promoting inequality, but all things that could contribute to the common good (for example, General Motors could be kept and transitioned to a nonprofit corporation, which it seems to be anyway).

Ah, but a man's reach should exceed his grasp,
Or what's a heaven for?
—Robert Browning[16]

Is it idealistic and unrealistic to strive for an egalitarian society? After all, one or another segment of humanity has been trying to build one for thousands of years. But the problem has been in trying to achieve freedom and equality by reforming hierarchies. That is a hopeless, impossible task! Look at the French Revolution. Its goals were marvelous: freedom, equality, brotherhood! The Revolution demolished the old hierarchy but created a new one, and a new one and a new one and…

Because all hierarchies are based on inequality, in the new society they cannot be the dominant form of organizational control. Organizational structures in the new society will be based on function. Any surviving hierarchies will be reorganized as networks, cooperatives, or associations. The connotations of "hierarchy" are too negative and could stimulate hypocrisy and regression.

The transition to the new society will involve millions of people finding the way of love in their own lives. During the transition, individuals can derive inspiration and support from *existing* activities, organizations, and achievements compatible with the new society.

An outstanding example, mentioned previously, is the "Universal Declaration of Human Rights." A stirring document that grew out of revulsion toward the horrors of World War II, it could have been a blueprint for the new society. But unfortunately, it called on the hierarchies of UN member states to implement its provisions. Its thirty articles (see appendix 1) can be used as a checklist to assess the achievements of the UN's members over the past sixty years—which have been woefully inadequate.

Note how many of the articles on human rights have been violated by government hierarchies around the world, including that of the United States, widely regarded as the globe's leading democracy. But despite these failures and violations, the declaration expresses the deep desires of people everywhere. All of its articles are supportive of the way of love and the new society. And each of us has the power to promote and act on many of them in our daily lives.

Contrast the inability of 192 governmental hierarchies to fully implement even one of their declaration's articles with the astounding success and worldwide impact of a single, private organization, Alcoholics Anonymous

(AA). The AA "program" consists of twelve steps leading to recovery from addiction (see appendix 2).[17] There is no hierarchy in local AA groups or in AA as a whole. The groups are autonomous, self-supporting, and self-governing, without any permanent officers. Membership and participation are purely voluntary.

From the perspective of hierarchy, AA should not work. But it does. Only seventy years old, it is the first successful program of recovery from alcoholism, a scourge with a history of thousands of years! AA has helped millions of individuals and families to transform their lives. And it demonstrates that hierarchy is not necessary to personal or social transformation.

Although AA does not formally promote freedom and equality, it works out that way in practice, and the transformative effect of the promotion of those values extends to members' relationships in the world beyond AA. The last phrase in the twelfth step is "and we practice these principles in all our affairs."[18] AA could well serve as a model for group action in the new society. It is self-described as a fellowship of men and women who share their experience, strength, and hope with each other so they may solve their common problems and help each other. From the perspective of the way of love, what better motto could there be for all of humanity?

An age-old institution that demonstrates how the freedom and equality of its members works effectively is the jury system. It is fundamental to our system of justice, although many people try to manipulate it or avoid it. Twelve strangers are given the power to decide on guilt or innocence, life or death, and multimillion dollar damages. Jury members may not be equal in circumstance, but they are free and equal as jurors. In their deliberations, there are disagreements, but the system works, and members are able to achieve the required consensus most of the time.

In 1976, the message of Marilyn Ferguson's *The Aquarian Conspiracy* was building on the increasing freedom and equality of the 60s and 70s, but was blunted by the conservative reaction that began at the same time. Like the articles of the UN's declaration, the principles espoused in her "conspiracy" are consistent with the new society. The transformative process Ferguson described is that of the way of love:

> Relationships are the crucible of the transformative process. They are bound to alter, given the individual's greater willingness to risk, trust in intuition, sense of wider connection with others, recognition of cultural conditioning…."The family," "marriage," and social relationships in general cannot be rethought by a committee or reformed by a program. These are not true institutions but millions upon millions of relationships—connections—that can only be understood at the level of the individual, and then only as a dynamic process.[19]

In discussing the character of future societies, Ferguson presented persuasive arguments for the eventual importance of networks in human activity. This was prescient—before the explosive growth of the Internet, which in its infancy has already changed the world and has now become the most important communication vehicle for networks. You may already be involved in this type of organization, which will be a hallmark of the new society. Each user is free and equal to every other, and has the ability to connect with every other, needing only their email address. There is no hierarchy.

Thousands of networks have already been created, both on the Internet and in the world at large, as nonhierarchical associations of volunteers who act in concert to pursue common goals and interests. They have no organizational structure beyond a communications center and connections to an amorphous membership, which may even be anonymous. A very large business could be similarly managed through an Internet network. This could be very important in the economic and political organizations of the new society.

In the United States, political networks have, in effect, made every local election into a national one through their ability to focus money and attention on critical races. Internet search engines have given everyone access to a world of information with the potential to provide literacy and education where none existed before. EBay has created a worldwide auction with worldwide price competition. YouTube enables anyone to broadcast personal videos to the world, creating havoc among politicians who find it more difficult to hide. In the near future, it is conceivable that individuals seeking public office will be able to communicate with millions of voters through the Internet without having to raise millions of dollars to pay for television time!

All of these developments provide greater political and economic power to people. However, in the evolution of the new society, these developments must be matched and supported by a flow of investment capital into activities that enhance the common good. Surprisingly, this is already well underway, as documented by the Social Investment Forum's 2007 *Report on Socially Responsible Investing Trends in the United States.*[20]

Between 1995 and 2005, socially responsible investing (SRI) in the United States grew from $639 billion to $2.71 trillion—an increase of 324 percent. Of the $25 trillion in total assets under management, the forum's 2007 report showed roughly 11 percent in SRI.[21] The organizations involved include major institutional investors (the California State Teachers' Retirement System), major industrial corporations (G. E. Ecomagination), traditional nonprofit organizations (Ford Foundation), and a new hybrid of for-profit activity supporting a nonprofit mission (the New Hampshire Community Loan Fund).

Some people call these hybrid organizations "the fourth sector," after government, business, and traditional nonprofits. Appendix 3 is a partial list of organizations with missions to promote the common good. This rapidly growing sector of the United States' economy shows great promise for redistributing wealth more fairly. As queried in the *New York Times* business section, "Could Altrushare or any other budding hybrid become another G. E.? Perhaps the better question is whether G. E. and other corporate titans could themselves become hybrids."[22]

Although small business drives the United States economy, most of the media hype has been about "Big Business." It has been extolled for years, and many of its past accomplishments were outstanding. But its recent performance raises questions as to whether bigness is beneficial anymore. The record includes failures such as AT&T, Enron, World Com, and Global Crossing Airlines, as well as corruption—Adelphia, Cendant, banks, and accounting firms.

We have seen enormous greed among CEOs and flagrant abuses of employees: layoffs, pension losses, 401(k) losses, and wage cuts everywhere except at the top. Big Business has also unjustifiably widened the gap between the wealthy and the middle class. It seems to reflect the government's Dr. Strangelove philosophy, "Let disaster wipe out the bottom. We'll survive!"

The purpose of human existence is not the accumulation of wealth, although some people believe it is and have even been willing to die for it. In the new society, motivation would not be solely economic. The world's productive capability would be expanded and humanity could develop more equitable patterns of distribution. Leading the way are those organizations currently involved in SRI and the fourth sector (see appendix 3). They are building the economic foundations of the new society.

Right now, we each have the ability to take actions to begin the transformation of society. We do not need a government or a religion or any other organization or institution to help us. Indeed, only individuals can take these actions to improve their personal relationships. No one can prevent them.

No one will be able to practice the way of love all the time. Sometimes we will be combating evil. Our goal is progress, not perfection. When our effort meets resistance, we can let it go. We will always have another opportunity. As the way of love spreads from person to person, it could be worldwide very quickly. Through the way of love, we can produce the new society—and fulfill the dream of poet Johann Wolfgang von Goethe: "If the whole world I once could see/On free soil stand, with the people free/Then to the moment might I say,/"Linger awhile...so fair thou art."[23]

We can create that moment. We have the brains. We have the power. The tools exist in society. It is up to us to do the work—to bring the way of love into our lives and create the new society.

Epilogue

We have so little time.

There is no "invisible hand" operating in society. Society is what we make it. The existing inequalities in society are personal products. Each of us has a hand in sustaining them. And they are moving us toward catastrophes that will occur within the next thirty or forty years—less than a single life span—unless we are able to achieve some fundamental changes in our relationships with each other.

The Earth and the universe will persist no matter what we humans do—whether our civilizations continue to exist or not, whether *we* continue to exist or not. Given the forces we have brought into play, our history could be one of the briefest of all species, or we can use our ingenuity once again to create a sustainable society in harmony with our environment and dedicated to the welfare of all humans.

In writing this book, I hoped it could contribute to the gradual transformation of human society from one based on inequality, individualism, and self-interest to one based on equality, altruism, and concern for the common good. There is ample evidence that this transformation has been underway for more than 200 thousand years in humanity's progress toward a "Type 1 civilization"[1] (see appendix 4).

A Type 1 civilization would be congruent with the new society and fulfill the irresistible human longing for freedom and equality.* This transformation involves such a fundamental shift in human thinking and behavior that it has necessarily been gradual—although, led by Western civilization, it greatly accelerated during the last millennium. And it may need to accelerate even more, because the continued advance of freedom and equality is threatened by the unintended consequences of humanity's successes: most notably, the consequences of our consumption of nonrenewable resources.

The consequences to be dealt with are population growth, the impact of environmental degradation on food production, and globalization. They comprise growing, irresistible forces that, for the most part, bode ill for the future of civilization. Worse, almost no government hierarchy is addressing the future impact of these problems on its own citizens, let alone the impact on humanity as a whole. In fact, no hierarchy has the inherent ability to deal with these world problems.

---

* Although personal freedom within the political and religious hierarchies of Western civilization has consistently improved from the Dark Ages (467–1100s) through the Age of Scholasticism (100s–1300s), Renaissance (1300s–1600s), Age of Reason (1600s), Age of Enlightenment (1700s), Age of Romanticism (1793–1815), and Age of Liberalism (1848–1914) to the present Age of Democracy, improvements in personal freedom were not freely given by the ruling hierarchies of any age. Rather, the hierarchies were forced to grant them, and the inequalities supporting the hierarchies' existence are still jealously guarded.

For example, at the Earth Summit of 1992 in Rio de Janeiro, the 178 participating nations agreed on an ambitious program of Official Development Assistance (ODA) called Agenda 21. Nineteen of the most developed reaffirmed a commitment to contribute 0.7 percent of their gross national income to ODA annually. But more than a decade later, none of the G-7* had met this target. France was the best of the group, contributing 0.41 percent in 2003, while the United States was the worst, at only 0.17 percent.[2]

This is not surprising, because hierarchies exist as autonomous, exclusive entities. When faced with an external threat, they must react in terms of the interests of their own constituencies or of their governing elite. Even alliances formed with other hierarchies to face a common threat must be based on self-interest. Therefore, a successful worldwide response to the global problems facing us can only come from a new society.

Each of these three most urgent problems facing civilization is an unintended consequence of the total impact of innumerable rational choices made by rational people. When a couple decides to have children, they do not consider the impact of their decision on world population. When farmers the world over (including agribusinesses) take steps to improve crop yields from exhausted, nutrient-deficient soils, they do not consider that they are reducing the stock of arable land and

---

* The G-7 is an association of seven industrialized nations formed in 1976: Canada, France, Germany, Italy, Japan, the United Kingdom, and the United States.

endangering future food production capacity. When entrepreneurs exploit opportunities to export goods and services to other countries, they do not consider that they are also exporting problems of success or failure to global economies.

And so it is that the economies of the world will need to deal with these problems during the next few decades. How they do it will determine the course of civilization for millennia. One possible scenario of peaceful cooperation involves continued globalization. Freed from limitations imposed by hierarchies, people and societies would likely develop innovative methods of production and consumption and actually help to correct the global imbalances in finance, energy consumption, and food production for the equitable support of future populations.

Already, the flow of investment capital to developing countries is increasing rapidly. The exploitation of such countries, once typified by colonialism, is being replaced by partnerships and joint ventures. In the future, these less-developed but resource-rich countries can benefit from competition between developed nations seeking access to their natural resources. This will be a positive effect of globalization.

Population growth. World population at midyear 1950 was just over 2.5 billion. At midyear 2006, world population was a little over 6.5 billion, an increase of 4 billion people in only 56 years! And at midyear 2050, world population is projected to be over 9.5 billion.[3] Think of it—all those people to be provided with water, food, clothes, housing, and the means of livelihood.

Population growth by itself is not the problem. The problem arises when the resources needed to support the lifestyle of the growing population exceed the "carrying capacity"* of the population's habitat—in this case, the Earth. Over a span of 200 thousand years, humans have repeatedly demonstrated the ability to increase the carrying capacity of their living space through ingenuity, innovation, and technology. No other species has this ability: when their habitats can no longer support them, they become extinct.

During our thousands of years as nomadic bands in Africa, we found new sources of food to support our growing populations through migration. We moved into new territories, eventually populating the world. Then, the introduction of agriculture made it possible to support many people in one place. Nomadism became a thing of the past and cities were born.

Agricultural productivity was increased through technology, e.g., the plow and irrigation. Human energy expended in planting and harvesting crops was enhanced by using animals that also produced fertilizer. Humans advanced from being mere consumers of renewable resources—hunters and gatherers—to being producers of renewable resources as well.

The next great advance in agricultural productivity followed the discovery and implementation of fossil fuels as humanity's primary energy source. Coal fueled the steam engine. Oil fueled the internal combustion engine and also stimulated the development of a whole new industry producing chemical fertilizer. In little more than 200 years, the use of fossil fuels has produced levels of production and consumption undreamed of when the

---

* Carrying capacity is "the maximum permanently supportable population of a habitat."[4]

United States was founded. It has also turned humanity back into hunters and gatherers, this time of *nonrenewable* resources, especially fossil fuels, which are becoming increasingly scarce.

Food is still the foundation of civilization, and it is unsettling to realize that food production is so dependent on the consumption of nonrenewable resources. It is not as if, when the supply of oil is gone, we can simply switch to something else. Right now, there is no "something else." And to feed 9.5 billion people in 2050—even at currently inadequate levels—world food production must increase by nearly 50 percent. Thus, the looming population problem involves a potentially unsustainable increase in demand, coupled with a deterioration of our ability to increase the supplies of food and oil.

Environmental degradation. Human activities have many adverse impacts on the environment. Housing encroaches on and destroys the habitats of other species. Disposal of waste products pollutes the air we breathe and the water we drink. However, my concern is focused on the particular factors in environmental degradation leading to the loss of arable land, thereby threatening future food production and the availability of safe drinking water.

These factors include the depletion of nonrenewable fossil fuels. Several others are related to poverty. The UN's Food and Agriculture Organization (FAO) emphasizes that hunger and poverty are linked to unsustainable practices and environmental degradation in a vicious cycle.[5] In the face of decreasing crop yields or persistent drought, poor farmers who lack access to knowledge or capital often resort to poor farming practices such as excessive cultivation, deforestation, and overgrazing. Other contributors to land loss are wind and water erosion, weed invasion, accelerating urbanization (e.g., buildings, roads, and highways), and the effects of global warming: loss of coastal lands to rising sea levels, saltwater incursion, changes in rainfall patterns, early snow melt—floods, then drought.

These factors have contributed to the world's presently enormous problems of hunger and malnutrition. According to the FAO, more than a billion people are suffering from hunger and an additional billion from malnutrition.[6]* That is nearly a third of the world's population, and the problem will worsen as current trends of population growth and arable land loss continue.

The yearly increase in world population is around 62 million,[7] and the yearly loss in arable land is about 10 million acres.[8] These figures mean that while the population to be fed is increasing by 170 thousand people each day, we are simultaneously losing the capacity to feed 330–380 thousand people daily,[9] or more than 120 million annually! That is a present-day disaster, yet world governments appear to be unwilling and unable to deal with it.

In the immediate future, an overhaul of the international humanitarian system is urgently needed but may not be made. As stated in Oxfam International's* 2009 report, *The Right to Survive*, "The humanitarian challenge of the twenty-first century demands a step-change in the quantity of resources devoted to saving

---

* "Hunger" is consuming less than 1,800–2,100 kilocalories a day. "Malnutrition" is having a diet deficient in micronutrients (such as vitamin A, iron, iodine, vitamin C, niacin, and thiamin).

* Oxfam International is a confederation of thirteen organizations working together in more than 100 countries to find lasting solutions to poverty and injustice.

lives in emergencies and in the quality and nature of humanitarian response. Whether or not there is sufficient will to do this will be one of the defining features of our age—and will dictate whether millions will live or die."[10]

Globalization—problem and solution. Globalization is not a neutral force. At its worst, globalization increases economic disparity when rich and powerful nations exploit those that are poorer and weaker: colonialism is the most shameful example. At its best, it reduces the economic disparity between rich and poor nations through fair trade.

Globalization began with commerce among nations, when businesses first sought to expand their operations beyond their countries of origin. Then, the process grew to include other aspects of national cultures: communication systems, technological developments, literature, arts, and ideas. All of this interaction was enabled by the increasing international flow of capital—the most mobile of all commodities. And facilitating the flow of capital is the flow of information. Already, an event in one nation is instantly known and its impact felt around the world.

Nations will be increasingly unable to exist in isolation or act unilaterally in visiting adverse consequences on other nations. Mutual accountability will bind the world together. Globalization—in both its negative and positive aspects—is providing the proof that we are indeed one world and one people.

Like population growth and environmental degradation, globalization is a process that cannot be controlled or stopped by any hierarchy. The nations of the world have become dependent on it. One example is the Internet, to which more than 1.5 billion people, a quarter of the human population, are connected. Some governments have tried to block access to some websites, but they cannot effectively block person-to-person communications.

No one knows the number or type of business and personal transactions conducted daily over the Internet, but it is surely in the trillions. This illustrates the most important positive effect of globalization—the leveling of imbalances in various aspects of world economies, resulting from innumerable transactions that are beyond the ability of any hierarchy (or anyone else) to control. Predatory economic practices will lose out to "fair trade" alternatives, which benefit trading partners equally.

Tipping points. The tipping point to correct the imbalance in global financing seems to have been reached already, with the recent collapse and continuing credit crisis brought on by the United States. Global financiers are seeking an alternative to the dollar as an acceptable reserve currency. In the not-distant future, the dominance of the dollar, or any other single currency, will be a thing of the past.

Tipping points to correct imbalances in other areas will also be reached in the near future. The next one will most likely be in the production and consumption of nonrenewable energy sources, especially oil and other fossil fuels, which are being rapidly depleted. Countries of the world must awaken to the seriousness of the problem. It will be a matter of survival. A global fuel shortage may be the tipping point that triggers survival responses—peaceful cooperation, or violent competition. Here again, the United States may feel the greatest impact because of its high levels of consumption.

Then will come the tipping point of the global

imbalance in food production and consumption. The food problem will be aggravated by the energy problem because of the heavy use of fossil fuels in making fertilizers. When less oil is available, there will be less chemical fertilizer, and declines in food production will worsen. A global food shortage is the most serious problem we will face.

With only 10 or 20 years left before we feel the first effects of these impending disasters, what positive actions can each of us take in the immediate future? We can adopt the way of love in our lives. We can begin to live with less, and more simply. We can support and promote the nongovernment organizations and the fourth-sector organizations that can help us transition to the new society. And finally, we can talk to each other about the evils and inadequacies of the hierarchies that control so much of our lives.

The problems ahead of us—population growth, environmental degradation, and globalization's fallout—resulted from trillions upon trillions of individual decisions. Likewise, the solution to these problems and the creation of an alternative society will also result from trillions upon trillions of individual actions. No hierarchy will provide the answer.

Acknowledgments

While I take full responsibility for the contents of this book, I need to recognize the substantial contributions made by three individuals to its quality. I am deeply indebted to all of them.

First, my friend, author Christina Crawford, read my initial manuscript, and her suggestions led to a restructuring of the book and significant revisions to its content. Next, my patient wife and collaborator, Barbara H. Hayes, PhD, pointed out several areas where more research and expanded treatment were needed to add to the power of the book. Finally, my editor, Kate Herman Johnson, in addition to her meticulous copyediting, was able to comprehend the meaning and intent of my writing. Of her many suggested revisions included in the book, I can only say, "Gee, I wish I'd said that!"

I also thank the following for permission to reproduce copyrighted material: AA World Services, Inc., Michael Shermer, *TIME* magazine, and the Publications Board of the United Nations Secretariat.

O. E. D.

Appendix 1

The Universal Declaration of Human Rights

Source: United Nations Secretariat Publications Board. http://www.un.org/Overview/rights.html. Reprinted by permission.

<u>Preamble</u>
Whereas recognition of the inherent dignity and of the equal and inalienable rights of all members of the human family is the foundation of freedom, justice, and peace in the world,

Whereas disregard and contempt for human rights have resulted in barbarous acts which have outraged the conscience of mankind, and the advent of a world in which human beings shall enjoy freedom of speech and belief and freedom from fear and want has been proclaimed as the highest aspiration of the common people,

Whereas it is essential, if man is not to be compelled to have recourse, as a last resort, to rebellion against tyranny and oppression, that human rights should be protected by the rule of law,

Whereas it is essential to promote the development of friendly relations between nations,

Whereas the peoples of the United Nations have in the Charter reaffirmed their faith in fundamental human rights, in the dignity and worth of the human person and in the equal rights of men and women and have determined to promote social progress and better standards of life in larger freedom,

Whereas Member States have pledged themselves to achieve, in co-operation with the United Nations, the promotion of universal respect for and observance of human rights and fundamental freedoms,

Whereas a common understanding of these rights and freedoms is of the greatest importance for the full realization of this pledge,

Now, Therefore THE GENERAL ASSEMBLY proclaims THIS UNIVERSAL DECLARATION OF HUMAN RIGHTS as a common standard of achievement for all peoples and all nations, to the end that every individual and every organ of society, keeping this Declaration constantly in mind, shall strive by teaching and education to promote respect for these rights and freedoms and by progressive measures, national and international, to secure their universal and effective recognition and observance, both among the peoples of Member States themselves and among the peoples of territories under their jurisdiction.

Article 1

All human beings are born free and equal in dignity and rights. They are endowed with reason and conscience and should act towards one another in a spirit of brotherhood.

Article 2
Everyone is entitled to all the rights and freedoms set forth in this Declaration, without distinction of any kind, such as race, colour, sex, language, religion, political or other opinion, national or social origin, property, birth, or other status. Furthermore, no distinction shall be made on the basis of the political, jurisdictional, or international status of the country or territory to which a person belongs, whether it be independent, trust, non-self-governing, or under any other limitation of sovereignty.

Article 3
Everyone has the right to life, liberty, and security of person.

Article 4
No one shall be held in slavery or servitude; slavery and the slave trade shall be prohibited in all their forms.

Article 5
No one shall be subjected to torture or to cruel, inhuman, or degrading treatment or punishment.

Article 6
Everyone has the right to recognition everywhere as a person before the law.

Article 7
All are equal before the law and are entitled without any discrimination to equal protection of the law. All are

entitled to equal protection against any discrimination in violation of this Declaration and against any incitement to such discrimination.

Article 8
Everyone has the right to an effective remedy by the competent national tribunals for acts violating the fundamental rights granted him by the constitution or by law.

Article 9
No one shall be subjected to arbitrary arrest, detention, or exile.

Article 10
Everyone is entitled in full equality to a fair and public hearing by an independent and impartial tribunal, in the determination of his rights and obligations and of any criminal charge against him.

Article 11
(1) Everyone charged with a penal offence has the right to be presumed innocent until proved guilty according to law in a public trial at which he has had all the guarantees necessary for his defence.
(2) No one shall be held guilty of any penal offence on account of any act or omission which did not constitute a penal offence, under national or international law, at the time when it was committed. Nor shall a heavier penalty be imposed than the one that was applicable at the time the penal offence was committed.

Article 12

No one shall be subjected to arbitrary interference with his privacy, family, home, or correspondence, nor to attacks upon his honour and reputation. Everyone has the right to the protection of the law against such interference or attacks.

Article 13

(1) Everyone has the right to freedom of movement and residence within the borders of each state.

(2) Everyone has the right to leave any country, including his own, and to return to his country.

Article 14

(1) Everyone has the right to seek and to enjoy in other countries asylum from persecution.

(2) This right may not be invoked in the case of prosecutions genuinely arising from non-political crimes or from acts contrary to the purposes and principles of the United Nations.

Article 15

(1) Everyone has the right to a nationality.

(2) No one shall be arbitrarily deprived of his nationality nor denied the right to change his nationality.

Article 16

(1) Men and women of full age, without any limitation due to race, nationality, or religion, have the right to marry and to found a family. They are entitled to equal rights as to marriage, during marriage and at its dissolution.

(2) Marriage shall be entered into only with the free and full consent of the intending spouses.

(3) The family is the natural and fundamental group unit of society and is entitled to protection by society and the State.

<u>Article 17</u>
(1) Everyone has the right to own property alone as well as in association with others.
(2) No one shall be arbitrarily deprived of his property.

<u>Article 18</u>
Everyone has the right to freedom of thought, conscience, and religion; this right includes freedom to change his religion or belief, and freedom, either alone or in community with others and in public or private, to manifest his religion or belief in teaching, practice, worship, and observance.

<u>Article 19</u>
Everyone has the right to freedom of opinion and expression; this right includes freedom to hold opinions without interference and to seek, receive, and impart information and ideas through any media and regardless of frontiers.

<u>Article 20</u>
(1) Everyone has the right to freedom of peaceful assembly and association.
(2) No one may be compelled to belong to an association.

<u>Article 21</u>
(1) Everyone has the right to take part in the government of his country, directly or through freely chosen representatives.

(2) Everyone has the right of equal access to public service in his country.

(3) The will of the people shall be the basis of the authority of government; this will shall be expressed in periodic and genuine elections which shall be by universal and equal suffrage and shall be held by secret vote or by equivalent free voting procedures.

Article 22

Everyone, as a member of society, has the right to social security and is entitled to realization, through national effort and international co-operation and in accordance with the organization and resources of each State, of the economic, social, and cultural rights indispensable for his dignity and the free development of his personality.

Article 23

(1) Everyone has the right to work, to free choice of employment, to just and favourable conditions of work, and to protection against unemployment.

(2) Everyone, without any discrimination, has the right to equal pay for equal work.

(3) Everyone who works has the right to just and favourable remuneration ensuring for himself and his family an existence worthy of human dignity, and supplemented, if necessary, by other means of social protection.

(4) Everyone has the right to form and to join trade unions for the protection of his interests.

Article 24

Everyone has the right to rest and leisure, including reasonable limitation of working hours and periodic holidays with pay.

Article 25

(1) Everyone has the right to a standard of living adequate for the health and well-being of himself and of his family, including food, clothing, housing, medical care, and necessary social services, and the right to security in the event of unemployment, sickness, disability, widowhood, old age, or other lack of livelihood in circumstances beyond his control.

(2) Motherhood and childhood are entitled to special care and assistance. All children, whether born in or out of wedlock, shall enjoy the same social protection.

Article 26

(1) Everyone has the right to education. Education shall be free, at least in the elementary and fundamental stages. Elementary education shall be compulsory. Technical and professional education shall be made generally available and higher education shall be equally accessible to all on the basis of merit.

(2) Education shall be directed to the full development of the human personality and to the strengthening of respect for human rights and fundamental freedoms. It shall promote understanding, tolerance and friendship among all nations, racial, or religious groups, and shall further the activities of the United Nations for the maintenance of peace.

(3) Parents have a prior right to choose the kind of education that shall be given to their children.

Article 27

(1) Everyone has the right freely to participate in the cultural life of the community, to enjoy the arts, and to share in scientific advancement and its benefits.

(2) Everyone has the right to the protection of the moral and material interests resulting from any scientific, literary, or artistic production of which he is the author.

Article 28
Everyone is entitled to a social and international order in which the rights and freedoms set forth in this Declaration can be fully realized.

Article 29
(1) Everyone has duties to the community in which alone the free and full development of his personality is possible.

(2) In the exercise of his rights and freedoms, everyone shall be subject only to such limitations as are determined by law solely for the purpose of securing due recognition and respect for the rights and freedoms of others and of meeting the just requirements of morality, public order, and the general welfare in a democratic society.

(3) These rights and freedoms may in no case be exercised contrary to the purposes and principles of the United Nations.

Article 30
Nothing in this Declaration may be interpreted as implying for any State, group, or person any right to engage in any activity or to perform any act aimed at the destruction of any of the rights and freedoms set forth herein.

Appendix 2

The Twelve Steps of Alcoholics Anonymous

Source: http://www.aa.org. Copyright © AA World Services, Inc. Reprinted by permission.

Alcoholics Anonymous is a fellowship of men and women who share their experience, strength, and hope with each other to solve their common problem and help other alcoholics to achieve sobriety.

These are the steps we took:

1. We admitted we were powerless over alcohol—that our lives had become unmanageable.
2. Came to believe that a Power greater than ourselves could restore us to sanity.
3. Made a decision to turn our will and our lives over to the care of God as we understood Him.

4. Made a searching and fearless moral inventory of ourselves.

5. Admitted to God, to ourselves, and to another human being the exact nature of our wrongs.

6. Were entirely ready to have God remove all these defects of character.

7. Humbly asked Him to remove our shortcomings.

8. Made a list of all persons we had harmed, and became willing to make amends to them all.

9. Made direct amends to such people wherever possible, except when to do so would injure them or others.

10. Continued to take personal inventory and when we were wrong promptly admitted it.

11. Sought through prayer and meditation to improve our conscious contact with God, as we understood Him, praying only for knowledge of His will for us and the power to carry that out.

12. Having had a spiritual awakening as the result of these Steps, we tried to carry this message to alcoholics, and to practice these principles in all our affairs.

Appendix 3

The Fourth Sector

The fourth sector consists of associations, programs, and corporations with a core commitment to social purposes embedded in their organizational structure and operating policies. They represent a transitional phase between the traditional, for-profit enterprise and the nonprofit, for-benefit enterprise of the new society.

Fourth-sector organizations are nongovernmental, and despite their many interrelationships, they are essentially independent entities. Financially self-sufficient, they attract investment capital from traditional and nontraditional sources. Furthermore, they demonstrate the ability of small groups of people to cooperate and successfully marshal resources to achieve specific, limited objectives that contribute to the common good.

Many examples of the fourth sector exist in the nonprofit realm, such as hospitals, colleges and universities, agricultural cooperatives, and condominium associations. The following samples illustrate the growing importance of the fourth sector in the United States and world economies, and the reader is urged to learn more about them. (Quotations are excerpted from the organizations' websites.)

ACCION
56 Roland Street, Suite 300, Boston, MA 02129
www.accion.org
"ACCION's mission is to give people the financial tools they need—microloans, business training, and other financial services—to work their way out of poverty."

Acumen Fund
76 Ninth Avenue, Suite 315, New York, NY 10011
www.acumenfund.org
"Business models capable of bringing affordable, life-changing products and services to parts of the world where markets have failed are now emerging. Launching a business that focuses on the needs of the world's poorest often seems impossible. Patient capital can make the difference in helping innovative business models that address poverty see the light of day." (Acumen Fund provides patient capital.)

Cafédirect
Unit F, Zetland House, 5-25 Scrutton Street, London, UK EC2A-4HJ
www.cafedirect.co.uk
"Our mission is to change lives and build communities through inspirational, sustainable business. We focus our social and economic impact on the developing world. We are the UK's largest 100% Fairtrade hot drinks company, and our work positively impacts the lives of 1.6 million people in 14 countries."

Community Sector Banking
Level 1, 251–253 Princes Highway, Corrimal, New South Wales, Australia 2518
www.csbanking.com.au
"Our mission is to enhance the capacity and capability of the community sector to deliver positive Social Impact through the creation and aggregation of capital. This is achieved by providing both banking and non-banking services and through the application of capital to projects and products that deliver positive social impacts."

The Global Exchange for Social Investment (GEXSI)
Brunnenstrasse 192, Berlin, Germany 10119
www.gexsi.org
"Our mission: to bring together charitable donors, social entrepreneurs, and social investors in funding exceptional economic, ecological, and social projects for sustainable development in low-income regions around the world."

Good Capital
901 Mission Street, Suite 105, San Francisco, CA 94103
www.goodcap.net
"Our first financial product, the Social Enterprise Expansion Fund, is seeking to fill the risk-taking expansion capital gap for social enterprise with an attractive blend of financial and social returns. Our innovative model enables a new class of investors to put their money to work to change the world."

Good Company Ventures
4700 Wissahickon Avenue, Philadelphia, PA 19144
www.goodcompanyventures.org
"Good Company Ventures is a community of service for

entrepreneurs developing for-profit businesses with social impact. It catalyzes start-ups with innovative solutions to big, unmet social needs."

Grameen Danone Foods
15 Rue du Helder, Paris Cedex 09, France 75439
www.danone.com
"The mission of Grameen Danone Foods speaks for itself: to reduce poverty by bringing health through food to children using a unique community-based business model. A joint venture launched by Danone and Grameen (the 'bank of the poor') in March, 2006, Grameen Danone Foods is a business—and as such must turn a profit—but its priorities are reversed. Grameen Danone Foods has placed social and environmental concerns at the heart of its business model. Although the company has to be profitable—profits from the first plants are needed to finance the construction of new plants—the success of the project will above all be judged on nonfinancial criteria: the number of direct and indirect jobs created (milk producers, small wholesalers, door-to-door sellers), improvements to children's health, protection of the environment, etc."

International Cooperative Alliance
15 Route des Morillons, Grand-Saconnex, Geneva, Switzerland 1218
www.coop.org
"Founded in 1895, the International Cooperative Alliance is an independent, nongovernmental organization which unites, represents, and serves cooperatives worldwide. It is the largest nongovernmental organization in the world. ICA's priorities center on promoting and defending the

Cooperative Identity, ensuring that cooperative enterprise is a recognized form of enterprise that is able to compete in the marketplace."

Investors' Circle
165 11th Street, San Francisco, CA 94103
http://investorscircle.net
"IC is a network of over 225 angel investors, professional venture capitalists, foundations, and family offices...using private capital to promote the transition to a sustainable economy. Since 1992, IC has facilitated the flow of over $134 million into more than 200 companies and small funds addressing social environmental issues. The IC20 is an index of the most successful and impactful companies that have received funding through the IC network since 1992. These companies stand as shining examples of the potential of social enterprise, proving that a focus on sustainability and social impact need not compromise profitability, and that socially responsible investment can result in substantial internal and external return."

Mondragon Corporation
Po Jose Ma Arizmendiarrieta No. 5, Mondragon, Guipuzkoa, Spain 20500
www.mondragon-corporation.com
The Mondragon Corporation is a federation of worker cooperatives owned by 85,066 worker-members. Power is based on the principle of one person, one vote. Currently, Mondragon is the seventh largest Spanish company in terms of revenue.
"In the Mondragon cooperatives, it is understood that Labour is the main factor for transforming nature, society, and human beings themselves. Capital is considered

to be an instrument, subordinate to Labour, which is necessary for business development. As a result, Labour is granted full sovereignty in the organization of cooperative enterprise, the wealth created is distributed in terms of the labour provided, and there is a firm commitment to the creation of new jobs. For many years, the difference in the payment received by the least qualified worker-member and the top executive of a cooperative was 1 to 3." (Recently, this ratio has been increased by worker-member vote to an average of 1 to 5.)

"On October 27, 2009, the United Steelworkers announced a framework agreement with Mondragon to develop unionized worker cooperatives in the manufacturing sector in the US."—*Amanda Wilson, "Bendable Business,"* The Dominion, *December 4, 2009*

New Hampshire Community Loan Fund
7 Wall Street, Concord, NH 03301
www.communityloanfund.org
"Our mission is to serve as a catalyst, leveraging financial, human, and civic resources to enable traditionally underserved people to participate more fully in New Hampshire's economy."

Opportunity International
2122 York Road, Suite 150, Oak Brook, IL 60523
www.opportunity.org
"Our vision is a world in which all people have the opportunity to provide for their families and build a fulfilling life. Our mission is to empower people to work their way out of chronic poverty, transforming their lives, their children's futures, and their communities. Opportunity International provides financial products

and strategies to over two million people working their way out of poverty in the developing world."

Partners for the Common Good
1801 K Street NW, Suite M-100, Washington, DC 20006
www.pcgloanfund.org
"Our vision is a world where low-income people have the means to support themselves and their families in dignity. Our lending activities facilitate affordable housing and neighborhood revitalization initiatives, improve the availability and quality of critical community services, promote entrepreneurship, and create economic opportunity for those often left out of the economic mainstream."

RSF Social Finance
1002-A O'Reilly Avenue, San Francisco, CA 94129
www.rsfsocialfinance.org
"RSF Social Finance frames all of its work in terms of an overarching Purpose informed by a set of core Values. The Purpose statement answers the question, 'Why do we exist?' The Values statement answers the question, 'What do we believe to be true?' Purpose: to transform the way the world works with money. Values: spirit…the primary role of money is to serve the highest intentions of the human spirit."

Skoll Foundation
250 University Avenue, Suite 200, Palo Alto, CA 94301
www.skollfoundation.org
"Our vision is to live in a sustainable world of peace and prosperity."
"Many of the problems of our modern world, ranging

from disease to drugs to crime to terrorism, derive from the inequities between rich and poor...rich nation vs. poor nation or rich community vs. poor community. It is in the best interests of the well-off to help empower those who are not as well-off to improve their lives."—*Jeff Skoll*

Social Investment Forum
910 17th Street NW, Suite 1000, Washington, DC 20006
www.socialinvest.org
An organization of 400 member firms dedicated to advancing the practice and growth of socially responsible investing (SRI; see chapter eight).

Social Venture Network
P.O. Box 29221, San Francisco, CA 94129
www.svn.org
"SVN inspires a community of business and social leaders to build a just economy and sustainable planet."

Appendix 4

Toward a Type 1 Civilization

Source: Michael Shermer, Los Angeles Times *July 22, 2008, p. 64. http://articles.latimes.com/2008/jul/22 /opinion/oe-shermer22. Reprinted by permission.*

Along with energy policy, political and economic systems must also evolve.

Our civilization is fast approaching a tipping point. Humans will have to make the transition from nonrenewable fossil fuels as the primary source of energy to renewable sources that will allow us to flourish into the future. Failure to make that transformation will doom us to the endless political machinations and economic conflicts that have plagued civilization for the last half-millennium.

We need new technologies to be sure, but without evolved political and economic systems, we cannot become what we must. And what is that? A Type 1 civilization. Let me explain.

In a 1964 article on searching for extraterrestrial

civilizations, the Soviet astronomer Nikolai Kardashev suggested using radio telescopes to detect energy signals from other solar systems in which there might be civilizations of three levels of advancement. Type 1 can harness all of the energy of its home planet; Type 2 can harness all of the power of its sun; and Type 3 can master the energy from its entire galaxy.

Based on our energy efficiency at the time, in 1973 the astronomer Carl Sagan estimated that Earth represented a Type 0.7 civilization on a Type 0 to Type 1 scale. (More current assessments put us at 0.72.) As the Kardashevian scale is logarithmic—where any increase in power consumption requires a huge leap in power production—we have a ways before 1.0.

Fossil fuels won't get us there. Renewable sources such as solar, wind, and geothermal are a good start and coupled to nuclear power could eventually get us to Type 1.

Yet the hurdles are not solely—or even primarily—technological ones. We have a proven track record of achieving remarkable scientific solutions to survival problems—as long as there is the political will and economic opportunities that allow the solutions to flourish. In other words, we need a Type 1 polity and economy, along with the technology, in order to become a Type 1 civilization.

We are close. If we use the Kardashevian scale to plot humankind's progress it shows how far we've come in the long history of our species from Type 0, and it leads us to see what a Type 1 civilization might be like.

- Type 0.1: Fluid groups of hominids living in Africa. Technology consists of primitive stone tools. Intra-group conflicts are resolved through dominance hierarchy, and between-group violence is common.

- Type 0.2: Bands of roaming hunter-gatherers that form kinship groups, with a mostly horizontal political system and an egalitarian economy.
- Type 0.3: Tribes of individuals linked through kinship but with a more settled and agrarian life style. The beginnings of a political hierarchy and a primitive economic division of labor.
- Type 0.4: Chiefdoms consisting of a coalition of tribes into a single beginnings of significant economic inequalities and a division of labor in which lower-class members produce food and other products consumed by non-producing upper-class members.
- Type 0.5: The state as a political coalition with jurisdiction over a well-defined geographical territory and its corresponding inhabitants, with a mercantile economy that seeks a favorable balance of trade in a win-lose game against other states.
- Type 0.6: Empires extend their control over peoples who are not culturally, ethnically, or geographically within their normal jurisdiction, with a goal of economic dominance over rival empires.
- Type 0.7: Democracies that divide power over several institutions, which are run by elected officials voted for by some citizens. The beginnings of a market economy.

- Type 0.8: Liberal democracies that give the vote to all citizens. Markets that begin to embrace a nonzero, win-win economic game through free trade with other states.
- Type 0.9: Democratic capitalism, the blending of liberal democracy and free markets, now spreading across the globe through democratic movements in developing nations and broad trading blocs such as the European Union.
- Type 1.0: Globalism that includes worldwide wireless Internet access, with all knowledge digitized and available to everyone. A completely global economy with free markets in which anyone can trade with anyone else without interference from states or governments. A planet where all states are democracies in which everyone has the franchise.

The forces at work that could prevent us from making the great leap forward to a Type 1 civilization are primarily political and economic. The resistance by nondemocratic states to turning power over to the people is considerable, especially in theocracies whose leaders would prefer we all revert to Type 0.4 chiefdoms. The opposition toward a global economy is substantial, even in the industrialized West, where economic tribalism still dominates the thinking of most politicians, intellectuals, and citizens.

For thousands of years, we have existed in a zero-sum tribal world in which a gain for one tribe, state, or nation meant a loss for another tribe, state, or nation—and our political and economic systems have been designed for use in that win-lose world. But we have the opportunity to live in a win-win world and become a Type 1 civilization by spreading liberal democracy and free trade, in which the scientific and technological benefits will flourish. I am optimistic because in the evolutionist's deep time and the historian's long view, the trend lines toward achieving Type 1 status tick inexorably upward.

That is change we can believe in.

Notes*

Preface

   1. Lemley. "Guth's Grand Guess."
   2. Ibid.
   3. Ibid.

Chapter 1

   1. Brand. "The Human Theater of the Absurd—II."
   2. Brand. "The Human Theater of the Absurd."
   3. MacLean. "Brain Roots of the Will-to-Power."
   4. Brand. "The Human Theater of the Absurd."
   5. MacLean. "Brain Roots of the Will-to-Power."
   6. Sagan. *The Dragons of Eden.*
   7. Ibid.
   8. MacLean. "Brain Roots of the Will-to-Power."
   9. Brand. "The Human Theater of the Absurd."
   10. MacLean. "Brain Roots of the Will-to-Power."

---

* See the bibliography for complete reference information.

11. Sagan. *The Dragons of Eden.*
12. Goudsblom et al. *The Course of Human History.*
13. Morrison and Severino. "Altruism."
14. Sagan. *The Dragons of Eden.*
15. Goudsblom et al. *The Course of Human History.*
16. Sagan. *The Dragons of Eden.*
17. Genesis 2:16–17. Holy Bible.
18. Sullivan. "When Grace Arrives Unannounced."

Chapter 2
1. Miller. *Sex and Gender Hierarchies.*
2. Peters. Editorial.
3. Deer. "Nature's Prey."
4. Zimmer. *Smithsonian Intimate Guide to Human Origins.*
5. Diamond. *Guns, Germs, and Steel.*
6. Smuts. "The Evolutionary Origins of Patriarchy."
7. Wrangham and Peterson. *Demonic Males.*
8. National Geographic Society. "Atlas of the Human Journey."

Chapter 3
1. Wrangham and Peterson. *Demonic Males.*
2. Ibid.
3. Reardon. "Pathways to Peace."
4. Ibid.
5. MacLean. "Brain Roots of the Will-to-Power."
6. Berle and Means. *The Modern Corporation and Private Property.*
7. Brand. "The Human Theater of the Absurd."
8. Brand. "The Human Theater of the Absurd—II."

9. Diamond. *Guns, Germs, and Steel.*
10. Diamond. *Collapse.*
11. UN Food and Agriculture Organization. "Statement to World Summit on Sustainable Development."
12. Moyers. "This Is the Fight of Our Lives."
13. Goodstein. "O Ye of Much Faith!"
14. Diamond. *Guns, Germs, and Steel.*
15. Bartlett and Steele. "How the Little Guy Gets Crunched."
16. Lincoln. Letter to William H. Herndon.
17. Gilbert. "Goering's Defense."
18. UN Secretariat Publications Board. "The Universal Declaration of Human Rights."

Chapter 4
1. Milgram. "The Perils of Obedience."
2. WGBH Educational Foundation. "Introduction."
3. Ibid. "One Friday in April, 1968."
4. Ibid. "An Unfinished Crusade."
5. Zimbardo. "The Power and Pathology of Imprisonment."
6. Ibid.
7. Ibid.
8. Ibid.
9. King, Jr. *Where Do We Go From Here.*

Chapter 5
1. Kelly. "Walt Kelly quotes."
2. Diamond. *Guns, Germs, and Steel.*
3. Wrangham and Peterson. *Demonic Males.*
4. Rummel. *Death by Government.*
5. Diamond. *Guns, Germs, and Steel.*

6. Woolley. *The Sumerians.*
7. Roux. *Ancient Iraq.*
8. Ibid.
9. Muhlberger. "War and Politics in Sumer and Akkad to the Time of Sargon."
10. Vail. "Defending Pala."
11. Powell. *Playing Life's Second Half.*
12. Lincoln. "Gettysburg Address."
13. Moyers. "This Is the Fight of Our Lives."
14. Ferguson. *The Aquarian Conspiracy.*
15. Ibid.

Chapter 6

1. Fricchione. "Separation, Attachment, and Altruistic Love."
2. McNulty. "From Single Cell to Full-Grown 'You.'"
3. Hardy. "Relationship, Involvement and Love."
4. Anderson. *The Stages of Life.*
5. Patterson. "The Speech Misheard Round the World."
6. Ibid.
7. Wheeler. "UCLA Researchers Identify the Molecular Signature of Loneliness."
8. King, Jr. Letter from Birmingham Jail.
9. Sagan. *The Dragons of Eden.*

Chapter 7

1. Teilhard de Chardin. "Pierre Teilhard de Chardin."
2. Morrison and Severino. "Altruism."
3. Boehm. *Hierarchy in the Forest.*
4. Ibid.

5. Sagan. *The Dragons of Eden*.
6. Bstan-'dzin-rgya-mtsho. *The Universe in a Single Atom*.
7. President's Council on Bioethics. *Human Cloning and Human Dignity*.
8. Brooks. "Longer Lives Reveal the Ties That Bind Us."
9. Niebuhr. "Reinhold Niebuhr."
10. Ibid.
11. Ferguson. *The Aquarian Conspiracy*.
12. Sagan. *The Dragons of Eden*.

Chapter 8
1. Fuller. "Richard Buckminster Fuller quotes."
2. Johnson. *Innovation*.
3. *Shakespeare Behind Bars*.
4. Ibid.
5. *OT*: Our Town Press Kit.
6. Ibid.
7. Ibid.
8. UN Secretariat Publications Board. "The Universal Declaration of Human Rights."
9. US Bureau of the Census. *Global Population at a Glance*.
10. Zakaria. "The Rise of the Rest."
11. Sagan. *The Dragons of Eden*.
12. Furedi. "The Sixties Myth."
13. Ibid.
14. Diamond. *Collapse*.
15. Sagan. *The Dragons of Eden*.
16. Browning. "Robert Browning quotes."
17. AA World Services. *Alcoholics Anonymous*.
18. Ibid.

19. Ferguson. *The Aquarian Conspiracy*.
20. Social Investment Forum. Executive summary.
21. Ibid.
22. Strom. "Businesses Try to Make Money and Save the World."
23. Von Goethe. "Johann Wolfgang von Goethe quotes."

Epilogue
1. Shermer. "Toward a Type 1 Civilization."
2. Gulasan. "Official Development Assistance."
3. US Bureau of the Census. *Global Population at a Glance*.
4. Catton. *Overshoot*.
5. UN Food and Agriculture Organization. "Statement to World Summit on Sustainable Development."
6. Ibid.
7. US Bureau of the Census. *Global Population at a Glance*.
8. Stevenson. "WorldClocks."
9. Ensminger and Ensminger. *Foods and Nutrition Encyclopedia*.
10. Oxfam International. Summary.

Bibliography

Alcoholics Anonymous World Services. *Alcoholics Anonymous: The Story of How Many Thousands of Men and Women Have Recovered from Alcoholism*. New York: Alcoholics Anonymous World Services, 1997.

Anderson, Clifford. *The Stages of Life: A Ground-breaking Discovery: The Steps to Psychological Maturity*. New York: Atlantic Monthly Press, 1995.

Ardrey, Robert. *African Genesis: A Personal Investigation into the Animal Origins and Nature of Man*. New York: Atheneum, 1965.

Baer, Greg. *The Truth About Relationships: A Simple and Powerfully Effective Way for Everyone to Find Real Love and Loving Relationships*. Rome, GA: Blue Ridge Press, 1998.

Barrow, John D. *The Book of Nothing: Vacuums, Voids, and the Latest Ideas About the Origins of the Universe*. New York: Random House, 2000.

Bartlett, Donald L., and James B. Steele. "How the Little Guy Gets Crunched." *TIME* February 7, 2000. http://www.time.com/time/magazine/article/0,9171,996000,00.html.

Berle, Adolf A., and Gardiner C. Means. *The Modern Corporation and Private Property.* New Brunswick, NJ: Transaction Publishers, 2007.

Boehm, Christopher. *Hierarchy in the Forest: The Evolution of Egalitarian Behavior.* Cambridge, MA: Harvard University Press, 2001.

Brand, John. "The Human Theater of the Absurd." *CommUnity of Minds* September 16, 2002. http://solutions.synearth.net/2002/09/16/.

———. "The Human Theater of the Absurd—II." *CommUnity of Minds* September 17, 2002. http://solutions.synearth.net/2002/09/17/.

Brooks, David. "Longer Lives Reveal the Ties That Bind Us." *New York Times* October 2, 2005. http://select.nytimes.com/2005/10/02/opinion/02brooks.html.

Browning, Robert. "Robert Browning quotes." ThinkExist.com Quotations, 2010. http://thinkexist.com/quotation/ah-but_a_man-s_reach_should_exceed_his_grasp-or/150975.html.

Bstan-'dzin-rgya-mtsho, Dalai Lama XIV. *The Universe in a Single Atom: The Convergence of Science and Spirituality.* New York: Morgan Road Books, 2005.

Catton, William R., Jr. *Overshoot: The Ecological Basis of Revolutionary Change*. Urbana: University of Illinois Press, 1980.

Coulter, Norman Arthur, Jr. *Synergetics: An Adventure in Human Development*. Englewood Cliffs, NJ: Prentice-Hall, 1976.

Deer, Brian. "Nature's Prey." *Sunday Times Magazine* (London) March 9, 1997, p. 5.

De Soto, Hernando. *The Mystery of Capital: Why Capitalism Triumphs in the West and Fails Everywhere Else*. New York: Basic Books/Perseus, 2003.

Diamond, Jared. *Collapse: How Societies Choose to Fail or Succeed*. New York: Viking, 2005.

———. *Guns, Germs, and Steel: The Fates of Human Societies*. New York: W. W. Norton, 1999.

———. *The Third Chimpanzee: The Evolution and Future of the Human Animal*. New York: HarperCollins, 1993.

Durant, Will. *The Story of Philosophy: The Lives and Opinions of the Greater Philosophers of the Western World*. New York: Simon & Schuster, 1961.

Dyson, Freeman J. *Infinite in All Directions*. New York: Harper & Row, 1988.

Elgin, Duane. *Voluntary Simplicity: Toward a Way of Life That Is Outwardly Simple, Inwardly Rich*. New York: William Morrow, 1993.

Ellis, George F. R. *Before the Beginning: Cosmology Explained*. New York: Boyars/Bowerdean, 1994.

Ensminger, Marion Eugene, and Audrey Ensminger. *Foods and Nutrition Encyclopedia*, 2nd ed., vol. 1. Boca Raton, Florida: CRC Press, 1993.

Farrell, Warren. *The Myth of Male Power: Why Men Are the Disposable Sex*. New York: Simon & Schuster, 1993.

Ferguson, Marilyn. *The Aquarian Conspiracy: Personal and Social Transformation in the 1980s*. Los Angeles: J. P. Tarcher, 1976.

————. *Aquarius Now: Radical Common Sense and Reclaiming Our Personal Sovereignty*. Boston: Weiser Books, 2005.

Foundation for Inner Peace. *A Course in Miracles*. New York: Viking Penguin, 1996.

Fricchione, Gregory L. "Separation, Attachment, and Altruistic Love: The Evolutionary Basis for Medical Caring." Chap. 20 in *Altruism and Altruistic Love: Science, Philosophy, and Religion in Dialogue*, edited by Stephen G. Post, Lynn G. Underwood, Jeffrey P. Schloss, and William B. Hurlbut, 346–61. New York: Oxford University Press, 2002.

Fuller, Richard Buckminster. "Richard Buckminster Fuller quotes." Goodreads, Inc., 2010. http://www.goodreads.com/author/quotes/165737.Richard_Buckminster_Fuller.

Furedi, Frank. "The Sixties Myth." *Spiked* August 3, 2004. http://www.spiked-online.com/Articles/0000000CA63F.htm.

Genesis 2:16–17. Holy Bible, New International Version (NIV). Biblica, 1984. http://niv.scripturetext.com/genesis/2.htm.

Gibbons, Ann. *The First Human: The Race to Discover Our Earliest Ancestors.* New York: Doubleday, 2006.

Gilbert, G. M. "Goering's Defense." *Nuremberg Diary.* New York: Farrar, Straus, 1947.

Goodstein, Laurie. "O Ye of Much Faith! A Triple Dose of Trouble." *New York Times* June 2, 2002, sec. 4, p. 5.

Goudsblom, Johan, Eric Jones, and Stephen Mennell. *The Course of Human History: Economic Growth, Social Process, and Civilization.* Armonk, NY, and London: M. E. Sharpe, 1996.

Grant, Colin. "Altruism: A Social Science Chameleon." *Zygon* 32, no. 3 (1997): 321–40.

Gulasan, Nergis. "Official Development Assistance: The Status of Commitments, Projections for 2010, and Preliminary 2009 Figures." United Nations Development Programme, 2010. http://www.undp.org/developmentstudies/docs/oda_april_2010.pdf.

Hardy, Arthur B. "Relationship, Involvement and Love." Unpublished paper. 1955.

Harrington, Michael. *The Other America: Poverty in the United States.* New York: Touchstone/Simon & Schuster, 1997.

Hoeller, Stephan A. *Freedom: Alchemy for a Voluntary Society.* Wheaton, IL: Theosophical Publishing House, 1992.

Johnson, Steven. "Innovation: It Isn't a Matter of Left or Right." *New York Times* October 30, 2010, p. BU-7.

Kaplan, Rabbi Aryeh. *Inner Space: Introduction to Kabbalah, Meditation and Prophecy.* Jerusalem: Moznaim Publishing, 1991.

Keeley, Lawrence H. *War Before Civilization: The Myth of the Peaceful Savage.* Oxford: Oxford University Press, 1997.

Kelly, Raymond C. *Warless Societies and the Origin of War.* Ann Arbor: University of Michigan Press, 2003.

Kelly, Walter. "Walt Kelly quotes." ThinkExist.com Quotations, 2010. http://thinkexist.com/quotation/we_have_met_the_enemy_and_he_is_us/227709.html.

Keniston, Kenneth. "Youth: A New Stage of Life." *American Scholar* 39 (1970): 631–54.

King, Martin Luther, Jr. Letter from Birmingham Jail, April 16, 1963. Birmingham, Alabama. http://coursesa.matrix.msu.edu/~hst306/documents/letter.html.

———. *Where Do We Go From Here: Chaos or Community?* Boston: Beacon Press, 1968.

Lemley, Brad. "Guth's Grand Guess." *Discover* 23, no. 4 (2002): 32–9.

Lincoln, Abraham. "Gettysburg Address." The Avalon Project. Yale Law School, Lillian Goldman Law Library, 2010. http://avalon.law.yale.edu/19th_century/gettyb.asp.

———. Letter to William H. Herndon, 15 February 1848. In *The Writings of Abraham Lincoln*, vol. 2, 1843–1858, p. 18. Classic Literature Library. http://www.classic-literature.co.uk/american-authors/19th-century/abraham-lincoln/the-writings-of-abraham-lincoln-02/ebook-page-18.asp.

MacLean, Paul D. "Brain Roots of the Will-to-Power." *Zygon* 18, no. 4 (1983): 359–74.

McNulty, Karen. "From Single Cell to Full-Grown 'You.' (Genetic Clues to Anatomical Development)." *Science World* 50, no. 12 (1994): 6.

Milgram, Stanley. "The Perils of Obedience." *Harper's Magazine* December 1973, pp. 62–77.

Miller, Barbara Diane (editor). *Sex and Gender Hierarchies*. Cambridge: Cambridge University Press, 1993.

Morrison, Nancy K., and Sally K. Severino. "Altruism: Toward a Psychobiospiritual Conceptualization." *Zygon* 42, no. 1 (2007): 25–40.

Moyers, William. "This Is the Fight of Our Lives." Keynote speech, Inequality Matters Forum, New York University, June 3, 2004. Published online June 16, 2004. http://www.commondreams.org/views04/0616-09.htm.

Muhlberger, Steven. "War and Politics in Sumer and Akkad to the Time of Sargon." Lecture 5, History 2055. Nipissing University, Ontario, Canada, 1998. http://www.nipissingu.ca/department/history/muhlberger/2055/l05anc.htm.

Murphy, Nancey, and George F. R. Ellis. *On the Moral Nature of the Universe: Theology, Cosmology, and Ethics.* Minneapolis: Augsberg Fortress, 1996.

National Geographic Society. "Atlas of the Human Journey." The Genographic Project, 2010. https://genographic.nationalgeographic.com/genographic/atlas.html.

Niebuhr, Reinhold. "Reinhold Niebuhr." BrainyQuote .com, Xplore, Inc., 2010. http://www.brainyquote.com/quotes/quotes/r/reinholdni100884.html, http://www.brainyquote.com/quotes/quotes/r/reinholdni162655.html.

OT: Our Town Press Kit. The Wilder Family, LLC, 2010. http://www.thorntonwilder.com/press-kit-for-ot-our-town.html.

Oxfam International. Summary. *The Right to Survive: The Humanitarian Challenge for the Twenty-First Century.* Oxfam International, April 2009. http://www.oxfam.org/sites/www.oxfam.org/files/right-to-survive-summary-eng.pdf.

Patterson, Orlando. "The Speech Misheard Round the World." *New York Times* January 22, 2005, sec. A. http://www.nytimes.com/2005/01/22/opinion/22patterson.1.html.

Peters, Karl E. Editorial. *Zygon* 17, no. 2 (1982):109–12.

Powell, David J. *Playing Life's Second Half: A Man's Guide to Moving from Success to Significance.* Oakland, CA: New Harbinger Publications, 2003.

President's Council on Bioethics. *Human Cloning and Human Dignity: An Ethical Inquiry.* Washington, DC, July 2002. http://bioethics.georgetown.edu/pcbe/reports/cloningreport/.

Reardon, Betty. "Pathways to Peace: The Creation of a Framework for a More Enduring World Peace: Making Peace a Real Possibility." Interview with John M. Whiteley, 1985. Social Ecology of Peace Series, University of California, Irvine. http://www.lib.uci.edu/quest/index.php?page=reardon/.

Roux, Georges. *Ancient Iraq.* New York: Penguin Books, 1992.

Rummel, R. J. *Death by Government.* New Brunswick, NJ: Transaction, 2004.

Sagan, Carl. *Broca's Brain: Reflections on the Romance of Science.* New York: Ballantine Books, 1980.

———. *Cosmos.* New York: Wings Books, 1983.

———. *The Dragons of Eden: Speculations on the Evolution of Human Intelligence.* New York: Ballantine Books, 1977.

———, and Ann Druyan. *Shadows of Forgotten Ancestors: A Search for Who We Are.* New York: Ballantine Books, 1993.

Shakespeare Behind Bars. Philomath Films, 2010. http://www.shakespearebehindbars.com.

Shermer, Michael. "Toward a Type 1 Civilization." *Los Angeles Times* July 22, 2008, p. 64. http://articles.latimes.com/2008/jul/22/opinion/oe-shermer22/.

Smithsonian National Museum of Natural History. "The Out of Africa Hypothesis" and "Genetic Evidence." The Human Origins Program Resource Guide to Paleoanthropology. http://anthropology.si.edu/humanorigins/faq/Encrta/encarta.htm.

Smuts, Barbara. "The Evolutionary Origins of Patriarchy." *Human Nature* 6, no. 1 (1995): 1–32.

Social Investment Forum. Executive summary. *2007 Report on Socially Responsible Investing Trends in the United States*. Washington, DC: Social Investment Forum, 2007.

Stevenson, John Harris. "WorldClocks: World Population and Productive Land Clock in Java-Script." Tranquileye, 2010. http://www.tranquileye.com/clock/.

Stringer, Chris, and Peter Andrews. *The Complete World of Human Evolution*. London: Thames & Hudson, 2005.

Strom, Stephanie. "Businesses Try to Make Money and Save the World." *New York Times* May 6, 2007. http://www.nytimes.com/2007/05/06/business/yourmoney/06fourth.html?pagewanted=all/.

Sullivan, Andrew. "When Grace Arrives Unannounced." *TIME* 165, no. 13, 2005. http://www.time.com/time/magazine/article/0,9171,1039693,00.html.

Teilhard de Chardin, Pierre. "Pierre Teilhard de Chardin." BrainyQuote.com, Xplore, Inc., 2010. http://www.brainyquote.com/quotes/quotes/p/pierreteil156689.html.

United Nations Food and Agriculture Organization. "Statement to World Summit on Sustainable Development, Johannesburg, 26 August–4 September 2002." United Nations, 2010. http://www.fao.org/docrep/003/y6265e/.

United Nations Secretariat Publications Board. "The Universal Declaration of Human Rights." United Nations, 2010. http://www.un.org/Overview/rights.html.

United States Bureau of the Census. *Global Population at a Glance: 2002 and Beyond.* International Programs Center, Population Division, Bureau of the Census. Washington, DC, March 2004. http://www.census.gov/prod/2004pubs/wp02-1.pdf.

Vail, Jeff. "Defending Pala: Rhizome as a Mode of Military Operations." *Rhizome* September 6, 2005. http://www.jeffvail.net/2005/09/defending-pala-rhizome-as-mode-of.html.

Von Goethe, Johann Wolfgang. "Johann Wolfgang von Goethe quotes." Goodreads, Inc., 2010. http://www.goodreads.com/quotes/show/58566/.

Wade, Nicholas. *Before the Dawn: Recovering the Lost History of Our Ancestors*. New York: Penguin Press, 2006.

Warren, Rick. *The Purpose Driven Life: What on Earth Am I Here For?* Grand Rapids, MI: Zondervan, 2002.

WGBH Educational Foundation. "Introduction," "One Friday in April, 1968," and "An Unfinished Crusade: An Interview with Jane Elliot, December 19, 2002." *Frontline: A Class Divided*. Broadcast March 26, 1985. Published online 2002. http://www.pbs.org/wgbh/pages/frontline/shows/divided/.

Wheeler, Mark. "UCLA Researchers Identify the Molecular Signature of Loneliness." *UCLA Newsroom* September 13, 2007. http://newsroom.ucla.edu/portal/ucla/Loneliness-Is-a-Molecule-UCLA-8214.aspx.

Woolley, C. Leonard. *The Sumerians*. New York: Barnes and Noble, 1955.

Wrangham, Richard, and Dale Peterson. *Demonic Males: Apes and the Origins of Human Violence*. Boston: Houghton Mifflin, 1996.

Zakaria, Fareed. "The Rise of the Rest: The Post-American World." *Newsweek* May 12, 2008, p. 27.

Zimbardo, Philip G. "The Power and Pathology of Imprisonment." U.S. House. Hearing before Subcommittee No. 3 of the Committee on the Judiciary, serial no. 15. *Corrections, Part II: Prisons, Prison Reform and Prisoner's Rights: California.* 92nd Cong., 1st sess., October 25, 1971. Washington, DC: U.S. Government Printing Office, 1971.

Zimmer, Carl. *Smithsonian Intimate Guide to Human Origins.* New York: HarperCollins, 2005.

Index

ForeWord Reviews

ForeWord Clarion Review

PHILOSOPHY

To Find the Way of Love: The Purpose of Our Existence
Oliver E. Deehan
AuthorHouse
978-1-4259-9851-6
Five Stars (out of Five Stars)

Oliver E. Deehan, a meticulous researcher and observer, seeks to show how love is the answer to human existence in *To Find the Way of Love: The Purpose of Our Existence*. For twenty years, Deehan has sought to understand humankind's place in the universe when it comes to life and love through science, the social sciences, theology, and philosophy. Deehan believes that the phenomenon of a monotheistic deity—in this case, God's existence—is in itself love. He draws from material by well-known authors, including Will Durant and Carl Sagan.

Deehan writes, "The importance of relationships in human affairs cannot be overstated. There is implicit recognition of this importance in our role designations . . . In all of these relationships, we as individuals must promote freedom and equality. That is the way of love."

While his explanation of love seems simple, its application is complex. We must first comprehend what Deehan calls "the fundamental and lasting ramifications of our common biological and physiological inheritance." When we put individualism before relationships, he believes, inequalities occur and surely evil will ensue. "Evil is a product of human society . . . Each of us is guilty of doing evil every time we support inequality in a relationship," he writers. "Evil is a matter of choice. It is an exercise in free will. This means man is not controlled by evil and does not need to choose it."

To Find the Way of Love is a small book, but it contains a wealth of information presented in a carefully researched and detailed fashion. The author makes a compelling case for altruism and equality in order for humanity to outpace the dinosaur's time on earth. Deehan merges science, economics, psychology, sociology, history, and theology into an accessible and easily understood treatise based on logic, common sense, and spirituality. Deehan's ideas for a "New Society" based on love will resonate with many people and could promote new ideas for a better world.

Lee Gooden

Deehan, Oliver E.
TO FIND THE WAY
OF LOVE
*The Purpose of Our
Existence*
AuthorHouse (206 pp.)
$15.95 Paperback
$9.99 e-book
July 26, 2011
ISBN: 978-1425998516

An awkward, somewhat New Age-y title doesn't begin to adequately serve this thorough analysis of human civilization and its primordial flaws.

Blame it on that pesky old reptilian brain and the ensuing hierarchies hatched in its wake. Be they familial, societal, governmental, religious or whatever else, Deehan convincingly traces the root of all evil to the myriad of stratified, top-down, command-and-control hierarchies that stubbornly persist to this day. The problem, according to the author, is that these manmade systems—so pervasive in our everyday lives—actually run counter to the intrinsic human need and desire for relationships rooted in freedom and equality. He calls this natural compulsion "love." Simply put, "love" works, inequity doesn't. As evidence, Deehan, a former hospital administrator and Navy fighter pilot, reaches all the way back to the very beginning and the Big Bang, where he finds proof of the inherent righteousness of collaboration in a rapidly cooling bowl of intergalactic "quark soup." After all, it was here that equal elemental particles were free to join up with whichever other particles they chose to in an unfathomable quest to create something greater than themselves. Concurring thoughts from pioneering thinkers such as Jared Diamond, Carl Sagan and others further underscore the thesis. Alas, the road mankind (under the undue influence of the self-serving brain) ultimately took was starkly different and probably had its roots in ancient Akkad, where readers are introduced to old king Sargon and his bloody, but ultimately fruitless, 150-year dynasty. The economy and ease in which the author is able to relate such scientific and historical data is commendable. The writing is clear and focused throughout. In this short yet profound work, hierarchy is the disease, and "love"—in the form of freedom and equality—is the cure. Sadly, one need only look at the profound challenges facing today's ego-driven, self-interested world to realize that.

An impressive foray into the inner workings of modern civilization—and how it might yet be saved from itself.

Kirkus Indie, Kirkus Media LLC, 6411 Burleson Rd., Austin, TX 78744
indie@kirkusreviews.com

About The Author

The author, Oliver E. Deehan was a Navy fighter pilot, sailor, skier, and executive who built and administered hospitals.

For the last 20 years, his concerns have been about human relationships and how the importance given to the individual has superceded the importance of relationships, with self-love trumping our love of others. This led to many years of thought, and a decade of researching and writing this book.

To find the way of love is to explore and reexamine the purpose of our existence.

CPSIA information can be obtained at www.ICGtesting.com
Printed in the USA
LVOW081229260212

270426LV00001B/1/P